Publisher's Note

Ancient Chinese classic poems are exquisite works of art. As far as 2,000 years ago, Chinese poets composed the beautiful work *Book of Poetry* and *Elegies of the South*. Later, they created more splendid Tang poetry and Song lyrics. Such classic works as *Thus Spoke the Master* and *Laws Divine and Human* were extremely significant in building and shaping the culture of the Chinese nation. These works are both a cultural bond linking the thoughts and affections of Chinese people and an important bridge for Chinese culture and the world.

Mr. Xu Yuanchong has been engaged in translation for 70 years. He won the Lifetime Achievement Award in Translation conferred by the Translators Association of China (TAC) in 2010, and won the "Aurora Borealis" Prize for Outstanding Translation of Fiction Literature, conferred by the Federation of International Translators (FIT) in 2014. He is honored as the only expert who translates Chinese poems into both English and French. After his excellent interpretation, many Chinese classic poems have been further refined into perfect English and French rhymes. This collection of Classical Chinese Poetry and Prose gathers his most representative English translations. It includes the classic works *Thus Spoke the Master, Laws Divine and Human* and dramas such as *Romance of the Western Bower, Dream in Peony Pavilion, Love in Long-life Hall* and *Peach Blooms Painted with Blood*. The largest part of the collection includes the translation of selected poems from different dynasties. The selection includes various types of poetry. The selected works start from the pre-Qin era to the Qing Dynasty, covering almost the entire history of classic poems in China. Reading these works is like tasting "living water from the source" of Chinese culture.

We hope this collection will help English readers "understand, enjoy and delight in" Chinese classic poems, share the intelligence of Confucius and Lao Tzu (the Older Master), share the gracefulness of Tang poems, Song lyrics and classic operas and songs and promote exchanges between Eastern and Western culture. We also sincerely invite precious suggestions from our readers.

出版前言

中国古代经典诗文是中国传统文化的奇葩。早在两千多年以前，中国诗人就写出了美丽的《诗经》和《楚辞》；以后，他们又创造了更加灿烂的唐诗和宋词。《论语》《老子》这样的经典著作，则在塑造、构成中华民族文化精神方面具有极其重要的意义。这些作品既是联接所有中国人思想、情感的文化纽带，也是中国文化走向世界的重要桥梁。

许渊冲先生从事翻译工作70年，2010年荣获"中国翻译文化终身成就奖"，2014年荣获国际译联颁发的"北极光"杰出文学翻译奖。他被称为将中国诗词译成英法韵文的唯一专家，经他的妙手，许多中国经典诗文被译成出色的英文和法文韵语。这套"许译中国经典诗文集"荟萃许先生最具代表性的英文译作，既包括《论语》《老子》这样的经典著作，又包括《西厢记》《牡丹亭》《长生殿》《桃花扇》等戏曲剧本，数量最多的则是历代诗歌选集。这些诗歌选集包括诗、词、散曲等多种体裁，所选作品上起先秦，下至清代，几乎涵盖了中国古典诗歌的整个历史。阅读和了解这些作品，即可尽览中国文化的"源头活水"。

我们希望这套许氏译本能使英语读者对中国经典诗文也"知之，好之，乐之"，能够分享孔子、老子的智慧，分享唐诗、宋词、中国古典戏曲的优美，并以此促进东西文化的交流。也敬请读者朋友提出宝贵意见。

PROJECT FOR TRANSLATION AND PUBLICATION
OF CHINESE CULTURAL WORKS

中国文化著作翻译出版工程项目

CLASSICAL CHINESE POETRY AND PROSE

300 TANG POEMS

TRANSLATED BY XU YUANCHONG

许译中国经典诗文集

唐诗三百首 ｜ 许渊冲 译

五洲传播出版社
China Intercontinental Press

中华书局
Zhonghua Book Company

CONTENTS
目　　　录

9

21

Bai Juyi

白居易

31

CLASSICAL CHINESE POETRY AND PROSE

300 TANG POEMS

TRANSLATED BY XU YUANCHONG

China Intercontinental Press   Zhonghua Book Company

PREFACE

It is said that the 21st century will be an age of globalization. The new generation worthy of the new age should be bred not only in its national culture but also in the global culture. Therefore, each nation should try to globalize its culture, in other words, to make its culture known to the world and become a part of the global culture so as to make it more brilliant.

If the 20th century may be said to be an American age, then the 19th was a British age and the 18th a French one. If we go further back, we may say that the 7th–13th centuries were Chinese ages, for during the Tang and the Song dynasties (618–1279), China was the most advanced country in the world, so far as political system, economic development and artistic and literary culture are concerned.

How did the Tang and the Song attain the highest development in the world during six hundred years? The answer may be summed up in two words, that is, the reign of "rite and music." According to professor Y. L. Feng, music imitates the harmony of nature and rite imitates the order of the universe. Rite is instituted to secure the mean in man's desire, and music, including poetry, to secure the mean in man's sentiment. Music is benevolence concretized and rite is justice externalized. If a state is governed with rite and music, its people will be just and benevolent, and the world will be peaceful and happy. That is one of the reasons why China has been standing among the great nations for thousands of years.

Emperor Xuan Zong (685–762) who reigned at the zenith of the Tang Dynasty enjoyed the highest economic and cultural prosperity when his government promoted the performance of rite and music. This may be seen from the first two verses he wrote when he offered sacrifice to Confucius in his temple:

How much have you done, O, my sage,

All for the good of all the age!

This shows how much he worshipped Confucius and admired his wisdom. He followed Confucius in imitation of the order of the universe and provided conditions to make the performance of rite and music possible.

Hence, Tang poetry has become a gem of traditional Chinese literature, As early as 1898, Herbert A Giles published his rhymed translations of Tang poems, of which Lytton Strachey said, "the poetry is it is the best that this generation has known," and that it "holds a unique place in the literature of the world" "through its mastery of the tones and depths of affection." Later, Arthur Waley said in his translations from the Chinese, "If one uses thyme, it is impossible not to sacrifice sense to sound," and he translated Tang poems into free verse. Thus began the controversy between rhymed version and free version in the translation of Chinese poetry. Generally speaking, the free translation emphasizes faithfulness to the original while the rhymed version, the beauty of the translated verse. Therefore, the controversy between these two types of translation may be said to be contradiction or conflict between faithfulness or truth and beauty. This controversy has lasted for a century. For instance, we may read the following versions of Li Bai's Farewell to a Friend. The first version is a word for word transliteration, the second is more faithful to the original in word while the third is more beautiful and poetical than the second.

(1) blue   hill   traverse   north   wall
    white   water   wind   east   town
    this   place   once   for   part
    lonely   thistledown   thousand   miles   journey
    float   cloud   roam   son   idea
    fall   sun   old   man   feeling
    wave   hand   from   here   go
    sough   spot   horse   neigh

(2) Green hills range north of the walled city,
    The White River curves along its east.
    Once we part here you'll travel far alone
    Like the tumbleweed swept by the autumn wind.
    A floating cloud — a wayfarer's feeling from home,
    The setting sun — the affection of an old friend.
    Waving adieu, as you now depart from me,
    Our horses neigh, loath to part from each other.

(3) Blue mountains bar the northern sky;
        White water girds the eastern town.
    Here is the place to say goodbye;

You'll drift like lonely thistledown.
With floating cloud you'll float away;
   Like parting day I'll part from you.
You wave your hand and go your way;
   Your steed still neighs, "Adieu, adieu!"

If we compare these versions, we may say the second is faithful to the original so far as words are concerned, and the third is as balanced as the first so far as lines are concerned. If we compare their diction, we may find "range" is a geographic term and "curve" a geometric one, and they are not so beautiful as "bar" and "gird," for the one may be found in Keats' verse "while barred clouds bloom the soft dying day." And the other may remind us of Edmund Waller's poem On a Girdle. What is more important is the third couplet. In the second version "feeling" and "affection" are used, these two words are rather prosaic. In the third we can find no such words but the repetition of "float" and "part," which cannot be found but implied in the original and which make the version more poetical. The same is true of the "adieu" in the last verse. These may be called creative translation or recreation, In the fourth line of the second version we find the tumbleweed "swept by the autumn wind," which cannot be found in the original either, Can it be called creative translation? If the poet compares his friend to tumbleweed "swept by the autumn wind," he implies that the friend is forced to leave the place, which is not the case. So I think the "swept" phrase should be considered as mistranslation. The difference between mistranslation and creative translation lies in whether the translator makes his version better or worse. A creative translator should make his reader understand and enjoy his version and even delight in it.

The difference between faithful translation and creative translation may be considered as contradiction between truth and beauty, or between science and art. Sometimes there is unity between them, that is the reason why Keats says, "Beauty is truth, truth beauty." But more often than not there is more contradiction than unity so far as verse translation is concerned. For instance, a couplet of Du Fu may be translated as follows:

(1) word for word transliteration:

   literature piece thousand ancient affair

   gain   loss   inch   heart   know

(2) A piece of literature is meant for the millennium.

   But its ups and downs are known already in the author's heart.

(3) A poem may long, long remain.

   Who knows the poet's loss and gain?

(4) A verse may last a thousand years.

   Who knows the poet's smiles and tears!

When we compare these four versions, we may find "a piece of literature" and "loss and gain" faithful to the original in words, and in these two cases may we say that there is unity between truth and beauty or between science and art. As Robert Frost said, poetry is "saying one thing and meaning another," so when

Du Fu said "a piece of literature," he meant a poem or verse, for he did not write much prose but poetry. So "a piece of literature" may be particularized into "poem" or "verse" here. As to "gain and loss," this phrase may either be generalized into "ups and downs" or particularized into "smiles and tears." Here we see more contradiction than unity in verse translation.

From the above examples we may conclude that the science school of translation emphasizes truth, that is, translation should be faithful to the original in word, in form and in sense, while the art school emphasizes beauty, that is, a translated verse should be as beautiful as the original in sense, in sound and in form. When a faithful version is not beautiful, we may use the methods of equalization (for example, millennium), generalization (long, long), and/or particularization (a thousand years) in order to make the reader understand and enjoy the version and delight in it. In short, the science school emphasizes understanding while the art school emphasizes enjoyment and delight.

Poetry, said Coleridge, is "the best words in the best order." If the equivalent in the translated text is not the best word, we may sacrifice the equivalent to the best, that is to say, we may make the fullest possible use of the best expressions in the target language. That is the reason why equalization, generalization and particularization are used, and that may be called creative translation or recreation. If the formula for the principle of science school is "1+1=2," then that for the theory of art school is "1+1>2."

For in science, the word goes as far as the sense, while in art, the sense goes beyond the word. Therefore, I think literary translation, and verse translation in particular, is not science but art.

In a certain sense, we may even say that literary translation is rivalry between the source language and the target language, to see which can better express the original idea. In reality, we may find such rivalry in the development of art and culture. For instance, the story of the Trojan war spread from mouth to mouth among the troubadours until Homer put it in words in the *Iliad*, so we may say that there was rivalry between the troubadours. Then Chapman in the 16th century and Pope in the 18th translated the *Iliad* from Greek into English, and there arose rivalry between the two languages. In a broader sense, even some of Shakespeare's works may be said to be resulted from rivalry. Was not *Hamlet* in rivalry with the Danish legend and *Romeo and Juliet* with the Venetian story? In the 17th century, Dryden rewrote Shakespeare's *Antony and Cleopatra* and his *All for Love* was said to have improved and surpassed Shakespeare. Was it not rivalry? Whether Dryden surpassed Shakespeare or not, opinions may differ and vary. But anyhow, there was rivalry between them, and it cannot be denied that human culture has made progress through rivalry.

300 Tang Poems are gems of Chinese literature. In 1929 Witter Bynner published his *Jade Mountains* in the United States, and in 1973 Innes Herdan published her translations in England. Both their versions are unrhymed: the former is more beautiful and the latter more faithful. In 1987 Hong Kong published a rhymed version of *300 Tang Poems*, which won high praises from critics, but some of the translated poems cannot be said to be faithful and beautiful. In 1994 my *Songs of the Immortals* was published by Penguin Books and my *Poetry of the South* was considered as a high peak even in English literature by an American scholar in Melbourne University. In 1998 Minerva press said my *Romance of the Western Bower* might vie with Shakespeare's *Romeo and Juliet* "in appeal and artistry." So I am asked to translate *300 Tang poems* to vie with English and American poets.

I have summed up my translation theories into the following words: "art of beautifulization and creation of the best as in rivalry." By "beautifulization" I mean a translated verse should be as beautiful as the original in sense, in sound and in form; by "ization" I include equalization (equivalence), generalization and particularization; by "ion" I imply comprehension (understanding), appreciation (enjoyment) and admiration (delight); by "creation" I understand the translator should be creative as the author of the original metamorphosed, writing and creating in the target language; by "the best" I mean an art of competition to see which version can better express the original idea, and make the reader understand and enjoy the poetry and delight in it.

There are a billion people who use the English language and more than a billion who use the Chinese, so these two languages are the most frequently used ones in the world, and the reciprocal translation between them is very important intercultural communication. As no people other than the Chinese have ever published a Chinese version of English or American masterpiece, so we have good reason to believe that our art of translation excels that of other nations in practice as well as in theory.

In 1988 dozens of Nobel Prize winners declared in Paris if mankind wish to perpetuate their existence, they must resort to Confucian wisdom. What is the wisdom of Confucius? Politically, it lies in the reign of "rite and music;" morally, it lies in the motto: "Do not do to others what you would not have others do to you;" literarily, it lies in the love of life, of nature, of peace, as shown in the *300 Tang Poems*. The love of peace shows the Confucian idea of "rite" or order, and the love of nature shows that of "music" or beauty. If the people of the 21st century should learn wisdom from Confucius and put it into practice, if they love peace and nature as the Tang poets did, then Confucian wisdom might benefit global civilization and people might live a more peaceful, more prosperous and happier life in the coming century.

Xu Yuanchong
October 19, 1999

Yu Shinan

TO THE CICADA

Though rising high, you drink but dew;
Yet your voice flows from sparse plane trees.
Far and wide there's none but hears you;
You need no wings of autumn breeze.

TO THE FIREFLY

Flickering, you shed a green light;
Wafting weak wings, you flit in flight.
Being afraid to be unknown,
In the darkness you gleam alone.

Kong Shao'an

FALLING LEAVES

In early autumn I'm sad to see falling leaves;
They're dreary like a roamer's heart which their fall grieves.
They twist and twirl as if struggling against the breeze;
I seem to hear them cry, "We will not leave our trees."

WANG JI

THE WINESHOP

Drinking wine all day long,
I won't keep my mind sane.
Seeing the drunken throng,
Could I sober remain?

A FIELD VIEW

At dusk with eastern shore in view,
I stroll but know not where to go.
Tree on tree tinted with autumn hue,
Hill on hill steeped in sunset glow.
The shepherd drives his herd homebound;
The hunter loads his horse with game.
There is no connoisseur around;
I can but sing of hermits' name.

HAN SHAN

LONG, LONG THE PATHWAY TO COLD HILL

Long, long the pathway to Cold Hill;
Drear, drear the waterside so chill.
Chirp, chirp, I often hear the bird;
Mute, mute, nobody says a word.
Gust by gust winds caress my face;
Flake on flake snow covers all trace.
From day to day the sun won't swing;
From year to year I know no spring.

SHANGGUAN YI

EARLY SPRING IN LAUREL PALACE

The royal cab leaves palace hall
For poolside garden 'mid sweet songs.
The trees are loud with orioles' call;
On vernal shore grass grows in throngs.
The breeze can write with morning dew;
'Neath blue sky flowers bloom like snow.
Butterflies come now and anew;
The hills are warmed by evening glow.

Wang Bo

FAREWELL TO PREFECT DU

You leave the town walled far and wide
For mist-veiled land by riverside.
I feel on parting sad and drear,
For both of us are strangers here.
If you have friends who know your heart,
Distance cannot keep you apart.
At crossroads where we bid adieu,
Do not shed tears as women do!

PRINCE TENG'S PAVILION

By riverside towers Prince Teng's Pavilion proud,
But gone are cabs with ringing bells and stirring strain.
At dawn its painted beams bar the south-flying cloud;
At dusk its uprolled screens reveal western hills' rain.
Leisurely clouds hang o'er still water all day long;
Stars move from spring to autumn in changeless sky.
Where is the prince who once enjoyed here wine and song?
Beyond the rails the silent river still rolls by.

YANG JIONG

I WOULD RATHER FIGHT

The beacon fire spreads to the capital;

My agitated mind can't be calmed down.

By royal order we leave palace wall;

Our armored steeds besiege the Dragon Town.

Darkening snow damages our banners red;

In howling winds are mingled our drumbeats.

I'd rather fight at a hundred men's head

Than pore o'er books without performing feats.

LUO BINWANG

THE CICADA HEARD IN PRISON

Of autumn the cicada sings;

In prison I'm worn out with care.

How can I bear its blue-black wings

Which remind me of my grey hair?

Heavy with dew, it cannot fly;

Drowned in the wind, its song's not heard.

Who would believe its spirit high?

Could I express my grief in word?

Wei Chengqing

PARTING WITH MY YOUNGER BROTHER

The long, long river coolly flows;

My parting sorrow endless grows.

Our grief is shared by falling blooms;

In their silence our sorrow looms.

Song Zhiwen

CROSSING RIVER HAN

I longed for news on the frontier

From day to day, from year to year.

Now nearing home, timid I grow;

I dare not ask what I would know.

Shen Quanqi

The Garrison at Yellow Dragon Town

'Tis said at Yellow Dragon Town
For years war has gone up and down.
Alas! at home wives watch the moon
Seen in the camp by men alone.
What would a young wife think in spring?
What dream last night did her man bring?
O, who with flags and drums could go
To take the town and beat the foe?

He Zhizhang

The Willow

The slender tree is dressed in emerald all about;
A thousand branches droop like fringes made of jade.
But do you know by whom these slim leaves are cut out?
The wind of early spring is sharp as scissor blade.

HOME-COMING

I left home young and not till old do I come back,

Unchanged my accent, my hair no longer black.

My children whom I meet do not know who am I.

"Where do you come from, sir?" they ask with beaming eye.

Since I left my homeland so many years have passed;

So much has faded away and so little can last.

Only in Mirror Lake before my oldened door

The vernal wind still ripples water as before.

CHEN ZI'ANG

ON THE TOWER AT YOUZHOU

Where are the great men of the past

And where are those of future years?

The sky and earth forever last;

Here and now I alone shed tears.

PARTING GIFT

The sword that cost me dear,
To none would I confide.
Now you are to leave here,
Let it go by your side.
Trees delight in spring day;
The pine loves wintry air.
What more need I to say?
Don't add to your grey hair!

ZHANG YUE

MY DELAYED DEPARTURE FOR HOME

My heart outruns the moon and sun;
It makes the journey not begun.
The autumn wind won't wait for me;
It arrives there where I would be.

LOOKING AT THE MOON AND LONGING FOR ONE FAR AWAY

Over the sea grows the moon bright;

We gaze on it far, far apart.

Lovers complain of long, long night;

They rise and long for the clear heart.

Candles blown out, fuller is light;

My coat put on, I'm moist with dew.

As I can't hand you moonbeams white,

I go to bed to dream of you.

SINCE MY LORD FROM ME PARTED

Since my lord from me parted,

I've left unused my loom.

The moon wanes, broken-hearted

To see my growing gloom.

ZHANG XU

TO A GUEST IN THE HILLS

On all things in the hills spring sheds a golden light.

Do not go back when some dark rain clouds come in sight!

Even on a fine day when the sun's shining bright,

Your gown will moisten still in the thick of clouds white.

LI LONGJI

SACRIFICE TO CONFUCIUS

How much have you done, O, my sage,

All for the good of all the ages!

Your offspring lives still on this land;

Your house and temple still there stand.

The phoenix deplored your sad state;

The unicorn foretold your fate.

We offer sacrifice to you,

For once you dreamed it was your due.

Zhang Ruoxu

The Moon over the River on a Spring Night

In spring the river rises as high as the sea,

And with the river's tide uprises the moon bright.

She follows the rolling waves for ten thousand *li*;

Where'er the river flows, there overflows her light.

The river winds around the fragrant islet where

The blooming flowers in her light all look like snow.

You cannot tell her beams from hoar frost in the air,

Nor from white sand upon the Farewell Beach below.

No dust has stained the water blending with the skies;

A lonely wheellike moon shines brilliant far and wide.

Who by the riverside did first see the moon rise?

When did the moon first see a man by riverside?

Many generations have come and passed away;

From year to year the moons look alike, old and new.

We do not know tonight for whom she sheds her ray,

But hear the river say to its water adieu.

Away, away is sailing a single cloud white;

On Farewell Beach are pining away maples green.

Where is the wanderer sailing his boat tonight?

Who, pining away, on the moonlit rails would lean?

Alas! the moon is lingering over the tower;

It should have seen her dressing table all alone.

She may roll curtains up, but light is in her bower;

She may wash, but moonbeams still remain on the stone.

She sees the moon, but her husband is out of sight;

She would follow the moonbeams to shine on his face.

But message-bearing swans can't fly out of moonlight,

Nor letter-sending fish can leap out of their place.

He dreamed of flowers falling o'er the pool last night;

Alas! spring has half gone, but he can't homeward go.

The water bearing spring will run away in flight;

The moon over the pool will in the west sink low.

In the mist on the sea the slanting moon will hide;

It's a long way from northern hills to southern streams.

How many can go home by moonlight on the tide?

The setting moon sheds o'er riverside trees but dreams.

WANG WAN

PASSING BY THE NORTHERN MOUNTAINS

My boat goes by green mountains high
And passes through the river blue.
The banks seem wide at the full tide;
A sail with ease hangs in soft breeze.
The sun brings light born of last night;
New spring invades old year which fades.
Where can I send word to my end?
Homing wild geese, fly westward, please!

WANG HAN

STARTING FOR THE FRONT

With wine of grapes the cups of jade would glow at night;
Drinking to pipa songs, we are summoned to fight.
Don't laugh if we lay drunken on the battleground!
How many warriors ever came back safe and sound?

Wang Zhihuan

ON THE STORK TOWER

The sun along the mountain bows;
The Yellow River seawards flows.
You will enjoy a grander sight
If you climb to a greater height.

OUT OF THE GREAT WALL

The Yellow River rises to the white cloud;
The lonely town is lost amid the mountains proud.
Why should the Mongol flute complain no willows grow?
Beyond the Gate of Jade no vernal wind will blow.

MENG HAORAN

LONGING FOR XIN THE ELDER

Suddenly daylight fades o'er western hill;
Gradually climbs the moon o'er eastern pool.
With windows open, at ease I lie still;
With hair unloosed, I enjoy evening cool.
The breeze brings fragrance from the lotus fair;
Dewdrops drip off bamboos with a splash clear.
I'd like to take my lute and play an air,
But I can find no connoisseur to hear.
How I long for you, my friend out of sight!
I wish you'd come in my dream at midnight.

PARTING FROM WANG WEI

Lonely, lonely, what is there to hope for?
Day after day I come back bare in heart.
I would seek fragrant grass in native shore.
How I regret with my old friend to part!
I'm one whom those in high place would elude,
For there are few connoisseurs in the state.
I can but keep myself in solitude
And go back to close my old garden gate.

VISITING AN OLD FRIEND'S COTTAGE

My friend's prepared chicken and rice;

I'm invited to his cottage hall.

Green trees surround the village nice;

Blue hills slant beyond city wall.

Windows open to field and ground;

O'er wine we talk of crops of grain.

On Double Ninth Day I'll come round

For the chrysanthemums again.

SPRING MORNING

This spring morning in bed I'm lying,

Not to awake till birds are crying.

After one night of wind and showers,

How many are the fallen flowers!

MOORING ON THE RIVER AT JIANDE

My boat is moored near an isle in mist grey;
I'm grieved anew to see the parting day.
On boundless plain trees seem to scrape the sky;
In water clear the moon appears so nigh.

LI QI

ARMY LIFE

We climb the hill by day to watch for beacon fires
And water horses by riverside when day expires.
We strike the gong in sand-darkened land where wind blows
And hear the pipa tell the princess' secret woe.
There is no town for miles and miles but tents in rows;
Beyond the desert there's nothing but rain and snow.
The wild geese honk from night to night, that's all we hear;
We see but Tartar soldiers shedding tear on tear.
'Tis said we cannot go back through the Jade Gate Pass;
We'd risk our lives to follow war-chariots, alas!
The dead are buried in the desert year by year,
Only to bring back grapes from over the frontier.

Wang Changling

Army Life

IV

Clouds on frontier o'er shadow mountains clad in snow;

A lonely town afar faces Pass of Jade Gate.

Our golden armor pierced by sand, we fight the foe;

We won't come back till we destroy the hostile state.

V

The wind and sand in the desert have dimmed sunlight;

With red flags half unfurled we go through the camp gate.

North of the River Tao, after nocturnal fight,

Our vanguards capture the chieftain of hostile state.

On the Frontier

The moon still shines on mountain passes as of yore.

How many guardsmen of the Great Wall are no more!

If the flying general were still there in command,

No hostile steeds would have dared to invade our land.

A NEGLECTED BEAUTY IN THE WEST PALACE

The lotus bloom feels shy beside the lady fair;

The breeze across the lake takes fragrance from her hair.

An autumn fan cannot conceal her hidden love;

In vain she waits for her lord with the moon above.

A DISFAVORED COURT LADY IN AUTUMN

At dawn she brings her broom to dust the golden halls;

She lingers with a fan within the palace walls.

Her rosy color envies wintry crows' black one,

Oft bathed in favorable light of royal sun.

SORROW OF A YOUNG BRIDE IN HER BOUDOIR

The young bride in her boudoir does not know what grieves;

She mounts the tower, gaily dressed, on a spring day.

Suddenly seeing by roadside green willow leaves,

How she regrets her lord seeking fame far away!

FAREWELL TO XIN JIAN AT LOTUS TOWER

A cold rain mingled with East Stream invades the night;

At dawn you leave the Southern hills lonely in haze.

If my friends in the North should ask if I'm all right,

My heart is free of stain as ice in crystal vase.

ZU YONG

SNOW ATOP SOUTHERN MOUNTAINS

How fair the gloomy mountainside!

Snow-crowned peaks float above the cloud.

The forest bright in sunset dyed,

With evening cold the town's o'er flowed.

WANG WEI

AT PARTING

Dismounted, I drink with you
And ask what you've in view.
"I can't do what I will,
So I'll go to south hill.
Be gone, ask no more, friend,
Let cloud drift without end!"

RURAL SCENE BY RIVER WEI

The village lit by slanting rays,
The cattle trail on homeward ways.
See an old man for the herd wait,
Leaning on staff by wicket gate.
Pheasants call in wheat field with ease;
Silkworms sleep on sparse mulberries.
Shouldering hoe, two ploughmen meet;
They talk long, standing on their feet.
For this unhurried life I long,
Lost in singing "Home-going song."

AUTUMN EVENING IN THE MOUNTAINS

After fresh rain in mountains bare
Autumn permeates evening air.
Among pine-trees bright moonbeams peer;
O'er crystal stones flows water clear.
Bamboos whisper of washer-maids;
Lotus stirs when fishing boat wades.
Though fragrant spring may pass away,
Still here's the place for you to stay.

MOUNT ETERNAL SOUTH

The highest peak scrapes the sky blue;
It extends from hills to the sea.
When I look back, clouds shut the view;
When I come near, no mist I see.
Peaks vary in north and south side;
Vales differ in sunshine or shade.
Seeking a lodge where to abide,
I ask a woodman when I wade.

HUNTING

Louder than gusty winds twang horn-backed bows;

Hunting outside the town the general goes.

Keener o'er withered grass his falcon's eye,

Lighter on melted snow his steed trots by.

No sooner is New Harvest Market passed

Than he comes back to Willowy Camp at last.

He looks back where he shot down vultures bare

Only to find cloud on cloud spread o'er there.

A VIEW OF THE RIVER HAN

Three southern rivers rolling by,

Nine tributaries meeting here.

Their water flows from earth to sky;

Hills now appear, now disappear.

Towns seem to float on rivershore;

With waves horizons rise and fall.

Such scenery as we adore

Would make us drink and drunken all.

ON MISSION TO THE FRONTIER

A single carriage goes to the frontier;
An envoy crosses northwest mountains high.
Like tumbleweed I leave the fortress drear;
As wild geese I come 'neath Tartarian sky.
In boundless desert lonely smokes rise straight;
Over endless river the sun sinks round.
I meet a cavalier at the camp gate;
In northern fort the general will be found.

THE CITY GATE

I've moved in near the city gate
Where withered willow trees are left.
Should another move here too late,
Alas! of trees he'd be bereft.

THE DEER ENCLOSURE

In pathless hills no man's in sight,
But I still hear echoing sound.
In gloomy forest peeps no light,
But sunbeams slant on mossy ground.

THE BAMBOO HUT

Sitting among bamboos alone,
I play my lute and croon carefree.
In the deep woods where I'm unknown,
Only the bright moon peeps at me.

THE DALE OF SINGING BIRDS

Sweet laurel blooms fall unenjoyed;
Vague hills dissolve into night void.
The moonrise startles birds to sing;
Their twitter fills the dale with spring.

PARTING IN THE HILLS

I see off the hills my compeer;

At dusk I close my wicket door.

When grass turns green in spring next year,

Will my friend come with spring once more?

OUR NATIVE PLACE

You come from native place;

What happened there you'd know.

Did mume blossoms in face

Of my gauze window blow?

LOVE SEEDS

Red berries grow in southern land.

How many load in spring the trees?

Gather them till full is your hand;

They would revive fond memories.

IN THE HILLS

White pebbles hear a blue stream glide;
Red leaves are strewn on cold hillside.
Along the path no rain is seen;
My gown is moist with drizzling green.

FAREWELL TO SPRING

From day to day man will grow old.
Enjoy the cup of wine you hold!
Don't grieve o'er flowers falling here;
They'll come with spring from year to year.

SONG OF AN AUTUMN NIGHT

Chilled by light autumn dew beneath the crescent moon,
She has not changed her dress though her silk robe is thin.
Playing all night on silver lute an endless tune,
Afraid of empty room, she can't bear to go in.

THINKING OF MY BROTHERS ON MOUNTAIN-CLIMBING DAY

Alone, a lonely stranger in a foreign land,

I doubly pine for my kinsfolk on holiday.

I know my brothers would, with dogwood spray in hand,

Climb up the mountain and miss me so far away.

A FAREWELL SONG

No dust is raised on the road wet with morning rain;

The willows by the hotel look so fresh and green.

I invite you to drink a cup of wine again;

West of the Sunny Pass no more friends will be seen.

SEEING A FRIEND OFF TO THE EAST

At willow-shaded ferry passengers are few;

Into the eastward stream the boatman puts his oars.

Only my longing heart looks like the vernal hue;

'T would go with you along northern and southern shores.

Liu Shenxu

A Scholar's Petreat

The pathway ends where rise clouds white;
Spring reigns as far as clear stream goes.
I oft see falling blooms in flight;
With endless waves their fragrance flows,
The path leads to the door oft shut;
A study's shad'd by willow trees.
From dazzling sun is screened the hut;
Soft light is filtered by the breeze.

Li Bai

The Moon over Mount Brow

The crescent moon looks like old Autumn's golden brow;
Its deep reflection flows with limpid water blue.
I'll leave the town on Clear Stream for three canyons now.
O Moon, how I miss you when you are out of view!

THE WATERFALL IN MOUNT LU VIEWED FROM AFAR

The sunlit Censer Peak exhales incenselike cloud;
Like an upended stream the cataract sounds loud.
Its torrent dashes down three thousand feet from high
As if the Silver River fell from the blue sky.

MOUNT HEAVEN'S GATE VIEWED FROM AFAR

Breaking Mount Heaven's Gate, the great River rolls through;
Green billows eastward flow and here turn to the north.
From both sides of the River thrust out the cliffs blue;
Leaving the sun behind, a lonely sail comes forth.

BALLAD OF A TRADER'S WIFE

My forehead barely covered by my hair,

Outdoors I pluck'd and played with flowers fair.

On hobby horse you came upon the scene;

Around the well we played with mumes still green.

We lived close neighbors on Riverside Lane,

Carefree and innocent, we children twin.

At fourteen years when I became your bride,

I'd often turn my bashful face aside.

Hanging my head, I'd look on the dark wall;

I would not answer your call upon call.

I was fifteen when I composed my brows;

To mix my dust with yours were my dear vows.

Rather than break faith, you declared you'd die.

Who knew I'd live alone in tower high?

I was sixteen when you went far away,

Passing Three Gorges studded with rocks grey,

Where ships were wrecked when spring flood ran high.

Where gibbons' wails seemed coming from the sky.

Green moss now overgrows before our door;

Your footprints, hidden, can be seen no more.

Moss can't be swept away, so thick it grows,

And leaves fall early when the west wind blows.

In yellow autumn butterflies would pass

Two by two in west garden o'er the grass.

This sight would break my heart and I'm afraid,

Sitting alone, my rosy cheeks would fade.

O when are you to leave the western land?

Do not forget to tell me beforehand!

I'll walk to meet you and not call it far

E'en to go to Long Wind Sands where you are.

PARTING AT A TAVERN IN JINLING

The tavern's sweetened when wind blows in willow-down;

A southern maiden urges guests to taste her wine.

My dear young friends have come to see me leave the town;

They who stay drink their cups and I who leave drink mine,

O ask the river flowing to the east, I pray,

Whether its parting grief or mine will longer stay!

PASSING BY THE TRIUMPHAL TOWER AT NIGHT

My boat sails down to River Town.

The Tower's bright in the moonlight.

The flowers blow like cheeks aglow,

And lanterns beam as fireflies gleam.

THOUGHTS ON A TRANQUIL NIGHT

Before my bed a pool of light—

Can it be hoar-frost on the ground?

Looking up, I find the moon bright;

Bowing, in homesickness I'm drowned.

SEEING MENG HAORAN OFF AT YELLOW CRANE TOWER

My friend has left the west where the Yellow Crane towers

For River Town veiled in green willows and red flowers.

His lessening sail is lost in the boundless blue sky,

Where I see but the endless River rolling by.

ENDLESS LONGING

I long for one in all at royal capital.

The autumn cricket wails beside the golden rails;

Light frost mingled with dew, my mat looks cold in hue.

My lonely lamp burns dull, of longing I would die;

Rolling up screens to view the moon, in vain I sigh.

My flowerlike Beauty is high up as clouds in the sky.

Above, the boundless heaven spreads its canopy screen;

Below, the endless river rolls its billows green.

My soul can't fly over sky so vast nor stream so wide;

In dreams I can't go through mountain pass to her side.

We are so far apart; the longing breaks my heart.

HARD IS THE WAY TO SHU

Oho! behold! how steep! how high!

The westward way is harder than to climb the sky.

Since the two pioneers

Put the kingdom in order,

Have passed forty eight thousand years,

And few have tried to pass its border.

Only birds could fly o'er White Mountains in the west,

And up to Mount Brows' crest.

After the mountain crumbled and road-builders died,

A rocky path was hacked along the mountain side.

Above stand peaks too high for dragons to pass o'er;

Below the torrents run back and forth, churn and roar.

Even the golden crane can't fly across;

How to climb over, gibbons are at a loss.

What tortuous mountain path Green Mud Ridge faces!

Around the top we make nine turns each hundred paces.

Looking up breathless, I could touch the stars nearby;

Beating my breast, I sink on the ground with a sigh.

When will you come back from this journey to the west?

How can you climb up dangerous path and mountain crest?

There you can hear on ancient trees but sad birds wail,

And see the male birds fly, followed by the female,

And hear home-going cuckoos weep

Beneath the moon in mountains deep.

The westward way is harder than to climb the sky.

On hearing this, your cheeks would lose their rosy dye.

Between the sky and peaks there seems less than a foot;

An old pine, head down, sticks into the cliff its root.

The cataracts and torrents vie in roaring loud;

Like thunder roll down frozen crags and boulders proud.

So dangerous these places are!

Alas! why should you come here from afar?

Rugged is the path between the cliffs so steep and high,

Guarded by one

And forced by none.

But disloyal guards

Might turn wolves and pards,

Man-eating tigers at daybreak

And at dusk blood- sucking serpent and snake.

You may find pleasure in the City of Brocade,

But it is better to go home, I am afraid.

The way to Shu is harder than to climb the sky,

I would turn westward and heave sigh on sigh.

HARD IS THE WAY OF THE WORLD

Pure wine in golden cup costs ten thousand coppers, good!

Choice dish in a jade plate is worth as much, nice food!

Pushing aside my cup and chopsticks, I can't eat;

Drawing my sword and looking round, I hear my heart beat.

I can't cross Yellow River: ice has stopped its flow;

I can't climb Mount Taihang: the sky is blind with snow.

I poise a fishing pole with ease on the green stream

Or set sail for the sun like the sage in a dream.

Hard is the way, hard is the way.

Don't go astray! Whither today?

A time will come to ride the wind and cleave the waves;

I'll set my cloudlike sail to cross the sea which raves.

A Faithful Wife Longing for Her Husband in Spring

With Northern grass like green silk thread,

Western mulberries bend their head.

When you think of home on your part,

Already broken is my heart.

Vernal wind, instruder unseen,

O how dare you part my bed-screen!

Deserted Beauty in Laurel Bower

Does Laurel Bower where grief reigns remember spring?

On the four golden walls the dusts of autumn cling.

The night holds up a mirror bright in the blue sky

To show the fair on earth as lonely as on high.

MIDNIGHT SONG — AUTUMN

Moonlight is spread all o'er the capital.

The sound of beating clothes far and near

Is brought by autumn wind which can't blow all

The longing away for far-off frontier.

When can we beat the foe on battleground

So that our men may come back safe and sound?

INVITATION TO WINE

Do you not see the Yellow River come from the sky,

Rushing into the sea and ne'er come back?

Do you not see the mirrors bright in chambers high

Grieve o'er the snow-white hair though once silk-black?

When hopes are won, O drink your fill in high delight,

And never leave your wine-cup empty in moonlight!

Heaven has made us talents, we're not made in vain.

A thousand gold coins spent, more will turn up again.

Kill a cow, cook a sheep and let us merry be,

And drink three hundred cupfuls of wine in high glee!

Dear friends of mine,

Cheer up, cheer up!

I invite you to wine.

Do not put down your cup!

I will sing you a song, please hear,

O hear! Lend me a willing ear!

Do not care for bells and drums, rare dishes you take!

I only want to get drunk and never to wake.

How many great men were forgotten through the ages?

But great drinkers are more famous than sober sages.

The prince of Poets feast'd in his palace at will,

Drank wine at ten thousand a cask and laughed his fill.

Why should a host complain of money he is short?

To drink with you I will sell things of any sort.

My fur coat worth a thousand coins of gold

And my flower-dappled horse may be sold

To buy good wine that we may drown the woe age-old.

DRINKING ALONE UNDER THE MOON

Among the flowers, from a pot of wine
I drink without a companion of mine.
I raise my cup to invite the Moon who blends
Her light with my Shadow and we're three friends.
The Moon does not know how to drink her share;
In vain my Shadow follows me here and there.
Together with them for the time I stay,
And make merry before spring's spent away.
I sing and the Moon lingers to hear my song;
My Shadow's a mess while I dance along.
Sober, we three remain cheerful and gay;
Drunken, we part and each may go his way.
Our friendship will outshine all earthly love;
Next time we'll meet beyond the stars above.

JOKING WITH DU FU

On top of Hill of Boiled Rice I met with Du Fu,
Who in the noonday sun wore a hat of bamboo.
Pray, how could you have grown so thin since we did part?
Is it because the verse-composing wrung your heart?

MOUNT SKYLAND ASCENDED IN A DREAM —
A SONG OF FAREWELL

Of fairy isles seafarers speak,

'Mid dimming mist and surging waves, so hard to seek.

Of Skyland southerners are proud,

Perceivable through fleeting or dispersing cloud.

Mount Skyland threatens heaven, massed against the sky,

Surpassing the Five Peaks and dwarfing Mount Red Town.

Mount Heaven's Terrace, five hundred thousand feet high,

Nearby to the southeast, appears crumbled down.

Longing in dreams for Southern Land, one night

I flew o'er Mirror Lake in moonlight.

My shadow's followed by moonbeams

Until I reach Shimmering Streams.

Where Hermitage of Master Xie can still be seen,

And clearly gibbons wail o'er rippling water green.

I put Xie's pegged boot

Each on one foot,

And scale the mountain ladder to blue cloud.

On eastern cliff I see

Sunrise at sea,

And in mid-air I hear sky cock crow loud.

The footpath meanders 'mid a thousand crags in the vale,

I'm lured by rocks and flowers when the day turns pale.

Bears roar and dragons howl and thunders the cascade;

Deep forests quake and ridges tremble: they're afraid.

From dark, dark cloud comes rain;

On pale, pale waves mists plane.

O lightning flashes

And thunder rumbles;

With stunning crashes

Peak on peak crumbles.

The stone gate of a fairy cavern under

Suddenly breaks asunder.

So blue, so deep, so vast appears an endless sky,

Where sun and moon shine on gold and silver terraces high.

Clad in the rainbow, riding on the wind,

The lords of clouds descend in a procession long,

Their chariots drawn by phoenix disciplined,

And tigers playing for them a zither song,

Row upon row, like fields of hemp, immortals throng.

Suddenly my heart and soul stirred, I

Awake with a long, long sigh.

I find my head on pillow lie

And fair visions gone by.

Likewise all human joys will pass away

Just as east-flowing water of olden day.

I'll take my leave of you, not knowing for how long,

I'll tend a white deer among

The grassy slopes of the green hill

So that I may ride it to famous mountains at will.

How can I stoop and bow before the men in power

And so deny myself a happy hour!

PAVILION LAOLAO

There is no place that oftener breaks the heart

Than the pavilion seeing people part.

The wind of early spring knows parting grieves,

It will not green the roadside willow leaves.

THE RUIN OF THE WU PALACE

Deserted garden, crumbling terrace, willows green,

Sweet notes of lotus songs cannot revive old spring.

All are gone but the moon o'er West River that's seen

The ladies fair who won the favor of the king.

THE RUIN OF THE CAPITAL OF YUE

The king of Yue returned, having destroyed the foe;

His loyal men came home, with silken dress aglow.

His palace thronged with flower-like ladies fair;

Now we see but a frock of partridges flying there.

SONG OF THE SOUTHERN MAIDEN

The waves of Mirror Lake look like moonbeam;

The maiden's fair as snow on waterside.

Her rippling dress vies with the rippling stream;

We know not which by which is beautified.

A REPLY

I dwell among green hills and someone asks me why;

My mind carefree, I smile and give him no reply.

Peach blossoms fallen on running water pass by;

This is an earthly paradise beneath the sky.

SOLITUDE

I'm drunk with wine

And with moonshine,

With flowers fallen o'er the ground

And o'er me the blue-gowned.

Sobered, I stroll along the stream

Whose ripples gleam.

I see no bird

And hear no word.

SITTING ALONE IN FACE OF PEAK JINGTING

All birds have flown away, so high;

A lonely cloud drifts on, so free.

Gazing on Mount Jingting, nor I

Am tired of him, nor he of me.

FAREWELL TO UNCLE YUN, IMPERIAL LIBRARIAN, AT XIE TIAO'S PAVILION IN XUANZHOU

What left me yesterday

Can be retained no more;

What troubles me today

Is the times I deplore.

For miles and miles the autumn breeze

Blows away the wild geese;

Let us drink our cups dry

In this pavilion high!

The prince of poets wrote with those in Fairy Isle,

And Junior Xie had his clear and spirited style.

We have the same ideal to fly

Up to the moon in the blue sky.

But when we cut water with sword, still it will flow;

When we drink to lighten grief, heavier it will grow.

If in this world we cannot drown our sorrow,

Then sail a boat with loosened hair tomorrow!

FAREWELL TO A FRIEND

Blue mountains bar the northern sky;

White river girds the eastern town.

Here is the place to say goodbye;

You'll drift like lonely thistledown.

With floating cloud you'll float away;

Like parting day I'll part from you.

You wave your hand and go your way;

Your steed still neighs, "Adieu, adieu!"

MY WHITE HAIR

Long, long is my whitening hair;

Long, long is it laden with care.

I look into my mirror bright:

From where comes autumn frost so white?

TO WANG LUN

I, Li Bai, sit aboard a ship about to go,

When suddenly on shore your farewell songs o'erflow.

However deep the Lake of Peach Blossoms may be,

It's not so deep, O Wang Lun! as your love for me.

LEAVING THE WHITE EMPEROR TOWN AT DAWN

Leaving at dawn the White Emperor crowned with cloud,

I've sailed a thousand miles through canyons in a day.

With monkeys' sad adieus the riverbanks are loud;

My skiff has left ten thousand mountains far away.

ASCENDING THE TOWER OF YUEYANG WITH XIA THE TWELFTH

The tower o'erlooks mountains on display;

The river stretches into the Lake of South.

The wild geese take our deep sorrow away;

The mountains throw the moon up from their mouth.

Make of white cloud a comfortable bed

And pass wine-cups around in the blue skies!

Drunken, let the cooling breeze rise and spread

Our sleeves dancing as flapping butterflies.

PASSING ONE NIGHT IN AN OLD WOMAN'S HUT AT THE FOOT OF MOUNT FIVE PINES

I lodge under the five pine trees;

Lonely, I feel not quite at ease.

Peasants work hard in autumn old;

Husking rice at night, the maid's cold.

Wild rice is offered on her knees;

The plate in moonlight seems to freeze.

I'm overwhelmed with gratitude.

Do I deserve the hard-earned food?

ELEGY ON MASTER BREWER JI OF XUANCHENG

For thirsty souls are you still brewing

Good wine of Old Spring, Master Ji?

In underworld are you not ruing

To lose a connoisseur like me?

ON DEATH BED

When flies the roc, Oh! he shakes the world;
His weakened wings, Oh! in midair are furled.
The wind he's raised, Oh! still stirs the sea;
He hangs his left wing, Oh! on sun-side tree.
Posterity mine, hear, O hear!
Confuscius dead, Oh! who'll shed a tear?

XU ANZHEN

MY NEIGHBOR'S LUTE

The Bear a thwart the sky, the night is waxing deep;
I gaze upon the moon, too sad to fall asleep.
Suddenly from the bower I hear a lute is played;
I know it must be she, my neighbor's lovely maid.
The music sweet reminds me of her eyebrows fair;
Her fingers must be cold when lively turns the air.
But her doors are locked for the eyes indiscreet,
So I cannot see her but in the dreamland sweet.

CUI HAO

YELLOW CRANE TOWER

The sage on yellow crane was gone amid clouds white.

To what avail is Yellow Crane Tower left here?

Once gone, the yellow crane will ne'er on earth alight;

Only white clouds still float in vain from year to year.

By sunlit river trees can be count'd one by one;

On Parrot Islet sweet green grass grows fast and thick.

Where is my native land beyond the setting sun?

The mist-veiled waves of River Han make me homesick.

SONGS ON THE RIVER

I THE WOMAN'S SONG

Where are you coming from?

On the shore I've my home.

Will you rest on your oar?

Are we from the same shore?

II THE MAN'S SONG

I dwell by riverside,

And sail on river wide.

We live on the same shore,

Not knowing it before.

Jin Changxu

A Lover's Dream

Drive orioles off the tree!
Their songs awake poor me
From dreaming of my dear
Far off on the frontier.

Cui Guofu

Waiting in Vain

I sweep the golden steps till they are clean,
And then I brush away the frost snow-white.
Alone I play my lute, drawing the screen.
How can I bear the autumn moon so bright?

Chang Jian

A BUDDHIST RETREAT BEHIND AN OLD TEMPLE IN THE MOUNTAIN

I come to the old temple at first light;

Only tree-tops are steeped in sunbeams bright.

A winding footpath leads to deep retreat;

The abbot's cell is hid' mid flowers sweet.

In mountain's aura flying birds feel pleasure;

In shaded pool a carefree mind finds leisure.

All worldly noises are quieted here;

I only hear temple bells ringing clear.

Gao Shi

Song of the Northern Frontier

A cloud of smoke and dust spreads over northeast frontier;

To fight the remnant foe our generals leave the rear.

Brave men should go no matter where beneath the sky;

The emperor bestows on them his favor high.

To the beat of drums and gongs through Elm Pass they go;

Round Mount Stone Tablet flags serpentine row on row.

But urgent orders speed over the Sea of Sand:

Mount Wolf aflame with fires set by the Tartar band.

Both hills and streams are desolate on border plain;

The Tartar horsemen flurry like the wind and rain.

Half of our warriors lie killed on the battleground,

While pretty girls in camp still sing and dance their round.

Grass withers in the desert as autumn is late;

At sunset few men guard the lonely city gate.

Imperial favor makes them hold the foemen light;

Their town is under siege, though they've fought with their might.

In coats of mail they've served so long on the frontiers;

Since they left home their wives have shed streams of impearled

tears.

In southern towns the women weep with broken heart;

In vain their men look southward, still they're far apart.

The northern front at stake, how can they go away?

On borders vast and desolate, how can they stay?

All day a cloud of slaughter mounts now and again;

All night the boom of gongs is heard to chill the plain.

Each sees the other's sword bloodstained in the hard strife.

Will they care for reward when they give up their life?

Do you not know

The bitterness of fighting with the foe?

Can they forget General Li sharing their weal and woe?

FAREWELL TO A LUTIST

Yellow clouds spread for miles and miles have veiled the day;

The north wind blows down snow and wild geese fly away.

Fear not you've no admirers as you go along!

There is no connoisseur on earth but loves your song.

Chu Guangxi

THE FISHING BAY

You may fish in late spring by lakeside green
Where apricot blossoms are running riot.
The lake seems shallow for its water's clean;
You see dispersed fish disturb lotus quiet.
You may wait at dusk for one you adore
And moor your boat by willow-shaded shore.

Liu Changqing

SEEKING SHELTER IN LOTUS HILL ON A SNOWY NIGHT

At sunset hillside village still seems far;
Cold and deserted the thatched cottages are.
At wicket gate a dog is heard to bark;
With wind and snow I come when night is dark.

SEEING OFF A RECLUSE

To the green temple 'mid bamboos
When evening bell rings, a recluse
Goes back alone. While sunset fills
His hat, he's lost in the blue hills.

ZHANG WEI

EARLY MUME BLOSSOMS

Like belts of white jade the cold-proof mume branches look,
Beside the pathway near the bridge over a brook.
If you don't know riverside blossoms early blow,
You would take them for last winter's unmelted snow.

Wan Chu

A Dancer at Dragon Boat Festival

Don't say the Western Beauty stands without a peer!
Today the Green Jade rivals Fair Blooms we revere.
Her eyebrows take the color from the verdant grass;
Her crimson skirt e'en pomegranite cannot surpass.
She sings a charming song and there's none but is charmed;
Her dance with captivating eyes makes all disarmed.
Who says the rainbow-hued threads can prolong our life?
Tonight I'll give it up for my love without strife.

Du Fu

Gazing on Mount Tai

O peak of peaks, how high it stands!
One boundless green o'erspreads two States.
A marvel done by Nature's hands,
O'er light and shade it dominates.
Clouds rise therefrom and lave my breast;
My eyes are strained to see birds fleet.
Try to ascend the mountain's crest:
It dwarfs all peaks under our feet.

SONG OF THE CONSCRIPTS

Chariots rumble

And horses grumble.

The conscripts march with bow and arrows at the waist.

Their fathers, mothers, wives and children come in haste

To see them off; the bridge is shrouded in dust they've raised.

They clutch at their coats, stamp the feet and bar the way;

Their grief cries loud and strikes the cloud

Straight, straightaway.

An onlooker by roadside asks an enrollee.

"The conscription is frequent," only answers he.

Some went north at fifteen to guard the rivershore,

And were sent west to till the land at forty-four.

The elder bound their young heads when they went away;

Just home, they're sent to the frontier though their hair's gray.

The field on borderland becomes a sea of blood;

The emperor's greed for land is still at high flood.

Have you not heard

Two hundred districts east of the Hua Mountains lie,

Where briers and brambles grow in villages far and nigh?

Although stout women can wield the plough and the hoe,

Thorns and weeds in the east as in the west o'ergrow.

The enemy are used to hard and stubborn fight;

Our men are driven just like dogs or fowls in flight.

"You are kind to ask me.

To complain I'm not free.

In winter of this year

Conscription goes on here.

The magistrates for taxes press.

How can we pay them in distress?

If we had known sons bring no joy,

We would have preferred girl to boy.

A daughter can be wed to a neighbor, alas!

A son can only be buried under the grass!"

Have you not seen

On borders green

Bleached bones since olden days unburied on the plain?

The old ghosts weep and cry, while the new ghosts complain;

The air is loud with screech and scream in gloomy rain.

TO LI BAI

When autumn comes, you're drifting still like thistledown;

You try to find the way to heaven, but you fail.

In singing mad and drinking dead your days you drown.

For whom will fly the roc? For whom will leap the whale?

EIGHT IMMORTAL DRINKERS (Excerpt)

Li Bai could turn sweet nectar into verses fine;

Drunk in the capital, he'd lie in shops of wine.

Even imperial summons proudly he'd decline,

Saying immortals could not leave the drink divine.

SONG OF THE FRONTIER

The bow you carry should be strong;

The arrows you use should be long.

Before a horseman, shoot his horse;

Capture the chief to beat his force!

Slaughter shan't go beyond its sphere;

Each State should guard its own frontier.

If an invasion is repelled,

Why shed more blood unless compelled?

ON THE WAY FROM THE CAPITAL TO FENGXIAN
(Excerpt)

The mansions burst with wine and meat;

The poor die frozen on the street.

Woe stands within an inch of weal.

Distressed, can I tell what I feel?

A MOONLIT NIGHT

On the moon over Fuzhou which shines bright,

Alone you would gaze in your room tonight.

I'm grieved to think our little children are

Too young to yearn for their father afar.

Your cloudlike hair is moist with dew, it seems;

Your jade-white arms would feel the cold moonbeams.

O when can we stand by the windowside,

Watching the moon with tears already dried?

SPRING VIEW

On war-torn land streams flow and mountains stand;

In vernal town grass and weeds are o'ergrown.

Grieved o'er the years, flowers make us shed tears;

Hating to part, hearing birds breaks our heart.

The beacon fire has gone higher and higher;

Words from household are worth their weight in gold.

I cannot bear to scratch my grizzling hair;

It grows too thin to hold a light hairpin.

LAMENT ALONG THE WINDING RIVER

Old and deprived, I swallow tears on a spring day;

Along Winding River in stealth I go my way.

All palace gates and doors are locked on rivershore;

Willows and reeds are green for no one to adore.

I remember rainbow banners streamed at high tide

To Southern Park where everything was beautified.

The first lady of the Sunny Palace would ride

In the imperial chariot by the emperor's side.

The horsewomen before her bore arrows and bow;

Their white steeds champed at golden bits on the front row.

One archer, leaning back, shot at cloud in the sky;

One arrow brought down two winged birds from on high.

Where are the first lady's pearly teeth and eyes bright?

Her spirit, blood-stained, could not come back from the height.

Far from Sword Cliff, with River Wei her soul flew east;

The emperor got no news from her in the least.

A man who has a heart will wet his breast with tears.

Would riverside grass and flowers not weep for years?

At dusk the rebels' horses overrun the town;

I want to go upward, but instead I go down.

COMING BACK TO QIANG VILLAGE

Like rugged hills hangs gilt-edged cloud;
The sunset sheds departing ray.
The wicket gate with birds is loud
When I come back from far away.
At my appearance starts my wife;
Then calming down, she melts in tears.
By chance I come back still in life,
While people drift in bitter years.
My neighbors look over the wall;
They sigh and from their eyes tears stream.
When night comes, candles light the hall;
We sit face to face as in dream.

ALONE I STAND

A falcon hovers in the sky;
A pair of gulls on water glide.
The falcon darts down from on high
On gulls floating on river wide.
The dewy grass may wet the wing;
The spider's net may trap the weak.
Nature and man are the same thing.
Aggrieved alone, I cannot speak.

FOR WEI THE EIGHTH

How rarely together friends are!
As Morning Star with Evening Star.
O what a rare night is tonight?
Together we share candlelight.
How long can last our youthful years?
Grey hair on our temples appears.
We find half of our friends departed.
How can we not cry broken-hearted!

After twenty years, who knows then,

I come into your hall again.

Unmarried twenty years ago,

Now you have children in a row.

Seeing their father's friend at home,

They're glad to ask where I come from.

Our talk has not come to an end,

When wine is offered to the friend.

They bring leeks cut after night rain

And millet cooked with new grain.

The host says, "It is hard to meet.

Let us drink ten cups of wine sweet!"

Ten cupfuls cannot make me drunk,

For deep in your love I am sunk.

Mountains will divide us tomorrow.

O What can we foresee but sorrow!

THE PRESSGANG AT STONE MOAT VILLAGE

I seek for shelter at nightfall.
What is the pressgang coming for?
My old host climbs over the wall;
My old hostess answers the door.
How angry is the sergeant's shout!
How bitter is the woman's cry!
I hear what she tries to speak out.
"I'd three sons guarding the town high.
One wrote a letter telling me
That his brothers were killed in war.
He'll keep alive if he can be;
The dead have passed and are no more.
In the house there is no man left,
Except my grandson in the breast
Of his mother, of all bereft;
She can't come out, in tatters dressed.
Though I'm a woman weak and old,
I beg to go tonight with you,
That I may serve in the stronghold
And cook morning meals as my due."
With night her voices fade away;
I seem to hear still sob and sigh.
At dawn again I go my way
And only bid my host goodbye.

DREAMING OF LI BAI

We stifle sobs on parting with the dead;

On parting with the living, tears are shed.

You're exiled to miasmic Southern shore.

How can you not send us news any more?

Last night you came into my dream anew;

This shows how long I am thinking of you.

Now you are caught in net and bound with strings.

How can you free yourself with bound-up wings?

I fear it was not your soul I did dream.

Could it go such long way o'er mount and stream?

When it came, green would maple forests loom;

When it went, dark mountains were left in gloom.

The setting moon on rafters sheds its light;

I seem to see your beaming face as bright.

O monstrous billows where water is deep,

Don't wake up monsters and dragons asleep!

THINKING OF MY BROTHER ON A MOONLIT NIGHT

War drums break people's journey drear;

A swan honks on autumn frontier.

Dew turns into frost since tonight;

The moon viewed at home is more bright.

I've brothers scattered here and there;

For our life or death none would care.

Letters can't reach where I intend;

Alas! the war's not come to an end.

TO MY SICK HORSE

You have been ridden long

Through cold, deep mountain pass.

In dust you toil along,

Sick at year's end, alas!

Is your coat not the same?

You are tame up to now.

Far dearer than your frame.

Can I not be moved? How?

TEMPLE OF THE PREMIER OF SHU

Where is the famous premier's temple to be found?
Outside the Town of Brocade with cypresses around.
In vain before the steps spring grass grows green and long,
And amid the leaves golden orioles sing their song.
Thrice the king visited him for the State's gains and pains;
He served heart and soul the kingdom during two reigns.
But he died before he accomplished his career.
How could heroes not wet their sleeves with tear on tear!

THE RIVERSIDE VILLAGE

The winding clear river around the village flows;
We pass the long summer by riverside with ease.
The swallow freely comes in and freely out goes;
The gulls on water snuggle each other as they please.
My wife draws lines on paper to make a chessboard;
My son knocks a needle into a fishing hook.
Ill, I need only medicine I can afford.
What else do I want for myself in my humble nook?

FOR A GUEST

North and south of my cottage winds spring water green;
I see but flocks of gulls coming from day to day.
The footpath strewn with fallen blooms is not swept clean;
My wicket gate is opened but for you today.
Far from market, I can afford but simple dish;
Being not rich, I've only old wine for our cup.
To drink together with my neighbor if you wish,
I'll call him o'er the fence to finish the wine up.

WRITTEN AT RANDOM

The river's broken-hearted to see spring pass away;
Standing on fragrant islet, I ask spring to stay.
But willow down runs wild and dances with wanton breeze;
Peach blossoms frivolous go with the stream as they please.

HAPPY RAIN ON A SPRING NIGHT

Good rain knows its time right;
It will fall when comes spring.
With wind it steals in night;
Mute, it moistens each thing.
O'er wild lanes dark cloud spreads;
In boat a lantern looms.
Dawn sees saturated reds;
The town's heavy with blooms.

MY COTTAGE UNROOFED BY AUTUMN GALES

In the eighth moon the autumn gales furiously howl;
They roll up three layers of straw from my thatched bower.
The straw flies across the river and spreads in shower,
Some hanging knotted on the tops of trees that tower,
Some swirling down and sinking into water foul.
Urchins from southern village know Im old and weak;
They rob me to my face without a blush on the cheek,
And holding armfuls of straw, into bamboos they sneak.
In vain I call them till my lips are parched and dry;
Again alone, I lean on my cane and sigh.

Shortly the gale subsides and clouds turn dark as ink;

The autumn skies are shrouded and in darkness sink.

My cotton quilt is cold, for years it has been worn;

My restless children kick in sleep and it is torn.

The roof leaks o'er beds, leaving no corner dry;

Without cease the rain falls thick and fast from the sky.

After the troubled times troubled has been my sleep.

Wet through, how can I pass the night so long, so deep!

Could I get mansions covering ten thousand miles,

I'd house all scholars poor and make them beam with smiles.

In wind and rain these mansions would stand like mountains high.

Alas! should these houses appear before my eye,

Frozen in my unroofed cot, content I'd die.

TO GENERAL HUA

With songs from day to day the Town of Silk is loud;

They waft with winds across the streams into the cloud.

Such music can be heard but in celestial spheres.

How many times has it been played for human ears?

A Playful Quatrain

Our four great poets write in a creative way;
You shallow critics may make your remarks unfair.
But your bodies and souls will fall into decay,
While their fame will last as the rivers flow fore'er.

Recapture of the Regions North and South of the Yellow River

'Tis said the Northern Gate is recaptured of late;
When the news reach my ears, my gown is wet with tears.
Staring at my wife's face, of grief I find no trace;
Rolling up my verse books, my joy like madness looks.
Though I am white-haired, still I'd sing and drink my fill.
With verdure spring's aglow, 'tis time we homeward go.
We shall sail all the way through Three Gorges in a day.
Going down to Xiangyang, we'll come up to Luoyang.

A QUATRAIN

Against blue water birds appear more white;

On green mountains red flowers seem to burn.

Alas! I see another spring in flight.

O when will come the day of my return?

A QUATRAIN

Two golden orioles sing amid the willows green;

A flock of white egrets flies into the blue sky.

My window frames the snow-crowned western mountain scene;

My door oft says to eastward-going ships "Goodbye!"

MOORING AT NIGHT

Riverside grass caressed by wind so light,

A lonely mast seems to pierce lonely night.

The boundless plain fringed with stars hanging low,

The moon surges with the river on the flow.

Will fame ever come to a man of letters

Old, ill, retired, no official life betters?

What do I look like, drifting on so free?

A wild gull seeking shelter on the sea.

THE STONE FORTRESS

With his exploits history is crowned;

For his Stone Fortress he's renowned.

The river flows but stones still stand,

Though he'd not taken back lost land.

ON THE RIVER

Each day upon the river falls cold rain;

The southern land in autumn looks forlorn,

The high wind blows down withered leaves again;

All night long I sit in my furs outworn.

No deeds achieved, in mirror oft I frown;

Unused for long, I lean on balustrade.

At this critical hour I'd serve the crown.

Though feeble, can I give up and evade?

ODE TO AUTUMN

The pearllike dewdrops wither maples in red dye;

The Gorge and Cliffs of Witch exhale dense fog around.

Waves of upsurging river seem to storm the sky;

Dark clouds o'er mountains touch their shadows on the ground.

Twice full-blown, asters blown off draw tears from the eye;

Once tied up, lonely boat ties up my heart home-bound,

Thinking of winter robes being made far and nigh,

I hear at dusk but nearby washing blocks fast pound.

ON THE HEIGHT

The wind so swift, the sky so wide, apes wail and cry;

Water so clear and beach so white, birds wheel and fly.

The boundless forest sheds its leaves shower by shower;

The endless river rolls its waves hour after hour.

A thousand miles from home, I'm grieved at autumn's plight;

Ill now and then for years, alone I'm on this height.

Living in times so hard, at frosted hair I pine;

Cast down by poverty, I have to give up wine.

ON RIVER HAN

On River Han my home thoughts fly,

Bookworm with worldly ways in fright.

The cloud and I share the vast sky;

I'm lonely as the moon all night,

My heart won't sink with sinking sun;

Autumn wind blows illness away.

A jaded horse may not have done,

Though it cannot go a long way.

ON YUEYANG TOWER

Long have I heard of Dongting Lake;

Now I'm on Yueyang Tower's height.

Here Eastern and Southern States break;

Here sun and moon float day and night.

No word comes from kinsfolk and friends;

A boat bears my declining years.

War is raging on the northern ends.

O what can I do but shed tears!

COMING ACROSS A DISFAVORED COURT MUSICIAN ON THE SOUTHERN SHORE OF THE YANGTZE RIVER

How oft in princely mansions did we meet!

As oft in lordly halls I heard you sing.

Now the Southern scenery is most sweet,

But I meet you again in parting spring.

CEN SHEN

SONG OF WHITE SNOW IN FAREWELL TO SECRETARY WU GOING BACK TO THE CAPITAL

Snapping the pallid grass, the northern wind whirls low;

In the eighth moon the Tartar sky is filled with snow

As if the vernal breeze had come back overnight,

Adorning thousands of pear trees with blossoms white.

Flakes enter pearled blinds and wet the silken screen;

No furs of fox can warm us nor brocade quilts green.

The general cannot draw his rigid bow with ease;

E'en the commissioner in coat of mail would freeze.

A thousand feet o'er cracked wilderness ice piles,

And gloomy clouds hang sad and drear for miles and miles.

We drink in headquarters to our guest homeward bound; With

Tartar lutes, pipas and pipes the camps resound.

Snow in large flakes at dusk falls heavy on camp gate;

The frozen red flag in the wind won't undulate.

At eastern gate of Wheel Tower we bid goodbye

On the snow-covered road to Heaven's Mountain high.

I watch his horse go past a bend and, lost to sight,

His track will soon be buried up by snow in flight.

SONG OF THE RUNNING HORSE RIVER IN FAREWELL TO GENERAL FENG ON HIS WESTERN EXPEDITION

Do you not see the Running Horse River flow

Along the sea of snow

And the sand that's yellowed sky and earth high and low?

In the ninth moon at Wheel Tower winds howl at night;

The river fills with boulders fallen from the height;

With howling winds they run riot as if in flight.

When grass turns yellow and plump Hunnish horses neigh,

West of Mount Gold dusts rise, the foe in proud array.

Our general leads his army on his westward way.

He keeps his iron armor on the whole night long,

Spears clang at midnight when his army march along,

Their faces cut by winds that blow so sharp and strong.

Their sweat and snow turn into steam on horse's mane,

Which soon on horse's back turns into ice again;

Ink freezes when challenge's written before campaign.

On hearing this, the foe with fear should palpitate.

Dare they cross swords with our brave men in iron plate?

We'll wait for news of victory at the western gate.

SPRING IN A DESERTED GARDEN

What riot do crows run, veiling the setting sun!

As far as eyes can see, there're two houses or three.

The garden trees don't know all men gone but the crow;

In full bloom they appear as when spring came last year.

ON MEETING A MESSENGER GOING TO THE CAPITAL

I look eastward, long, long my homeward road appears.

My old arms tremble and my sleeves are wet with tears.

Meeting you on horseback, with what brush can I write?

I can but ask you to tell them I am all right.

SPRING DREAM

The vernal breeze in inner chamber rose last night;
I remembered my fair one was by riverside.
An hour on pillow I dreamed of passing in flight
Thousands of miles to Southern shore where she'd abide.

JIA ZHI

SPRING THOUGHTS

The yellow willows wave above, green grass below;
Peach blooms run riot and plum blossoms fragrant grow.
The vernal wind cannot blow my sorrow away;
My grief increases with each lengthening spring day.

BOATING WITH LI BAI AND PEI DI ON LAKE DONGTING

Shower by shower fall lakeside maple leaves drear;
Lake Dongting's rippled by autumn breeze towards night.
We sail at will, careless if we've gone far or near,
To mourn o'er Beauties drowned with the moon and clouds white.

Yuan Jie

Drinking on Stone Fish Lake

On Stone Fish Lake as on Dongting I gaze my fill
On brimming summer water as on verdant hill.
Using the vale as cup and water as wine pools,
The tipplers sit on rocks as cosy as on stools.
The wind so strong has formed great waves from day to day;
It can't prevent the boats from bringing wine this way.
A ladle in my hand, I sit on rocky shore;
To do away with care, we drink the wine I pour.

Liu Fangping

A Moonlit Night

The moon has brightened half the house at dead of night;
The slanting Plough and Southern stars shed dying light.
I feel the warmth of air exhaled by coming spring
For through my window screen I hear the insects sing.

LONELINESS

Out of the window wanes twilight of parting day;

None sees her dry her furtive tears in gilded hall.

In lonely courtyard even spring will pass away;

She won't open the door but lets pear blossoms fall.

SIKONG SHU

REVERIE IN A RIVERSIDE VILLAGE

Coming back from fishing, I don't fasten my boat;

The moon sinks o'er riverside village — time to sleep.

What if the breeze at night should set my skiff afloat?

It's still amid the reeds, where water is not deep.

FAREWELL TO A FRIEND

Although I know that we shall meet again,

How can we bear to part on such a night?

Do you think wine and friendship can't retain

You here longer than an adverse wind might?

QIAN QI

TO THE RETURNING WILD GEESE

Wild geese, why don't you stay there anymore
With blue water, bright sand and mossy shore?
The moonbeams play on twenty-five sad strings.
Can you not bear the grief the zither brings?

GU KUANG

A PALACE POEM

From the jade bower songs float halfway up the sky;
The wind carries the palace maids' gay voices high.
The moon is slanting, drips of water-clock are heard;
The screen uprolled, the weaver's seen far from the cowherd.

ZHANG JI

MOORING BY MAPLE BRIDGE AT NIGHT

At moonset cry the crows, streaking the frosty sky;
Dimly lit fishing boats 'neath maples sadly lie.
Beyond the city wall, from Temple of Cold Hill
Bells break the ship-borne roamer's dream and midnight still.

Han Hong

COLD FOOD DAY

Nowhere in vernal town but sweet flowers fly down;

Riverside willow trees slant in the eastern breeze.

At dusk the palace sends privilege candles red

To the five lordly mansions where wreaths of smoke spread.

Wei Yingwu

TO A HERMIT ON AN AUTUMN NIGHT

Strolling when autumn night is still,

I think of you and softly sing.

As pine cones fall in empty hill,

Hermit, you must be listening.

ON THE WEST STREAM AT CHUZHOU

Alone, I like the riverside where green grass grows

And golden orioles sing amid the leafy trees.

When showers fall at dusk, the river overflows;

A lonely boat athwart the ferry floats at ease.

GENG WEI

A LONELY AUTUMN DAY

O'er the lane slants the sun;
I'm grieved but can tell none.
On ancient way none goes;
O'er cornfields west wind blows.

LU LUN

GRIEF IN AUTUMN

As years pass by, grey grows my hair;
When autumn's come, the trees stand bare.
Perplexed, I ask the yellow leaf,
"Is your heart like mine gnawed by grief?"

BORDER SONGS

I

His arrow tuft'd with vulture feather,

His pennon shaped like swallowtail.

He gives an order out; together

A thousand battalions shout, "Hail!"

II

In gloomy woods grass shivers at wind's howl;

The general takes it for a tiger's growl.

He shoots and looks for his arrow next morn

Only to find a rock pierced 'mid the thorn.

III

Wild geese fly high in moonless night;

The Tartars through the dark take flight.

Our horsemen chase them, armed with bow

And sword covered with heavy snow.

IV

Let sumptuous banquet in the wild be spread!

Let tribesmen give the victors warm welcome!

Let's dance in golden armor, drunk and fed!

Let mountains tremble at thunderous drum!

Li Yi

MEETING AND PARTING WITH MY COUSIN

We parted for ten war-torn years;

Not till grown up do we meet again.

At first I think a stranger appears;

Your name reminds me of your face then.

We talk of changeful night and day

Until we hear the evening bell.

Tomorrow you'll go southward way

O'er autumn hills. O, fare you well!

GRIEF OF A PALACE MAID

Spring palace fragrant with sweet flowers wet with dew

Is ringing with flute songs when the moon's shining bright.

The water-clock seems filled up with the ocean blue

To make the night appear for me an endless night.

ON HEARING A FLUTE AT NIGHT ATOP THE VICTOR'S WALL

Below the beacon tower sand looks white as snow;

Beyond the Victor's Wall like frost cold moonbeams flow.

None knows from where a flute blows a nostalgic song;

All warriors lie awake homesick the whole night long.

A SOUTHERN SONG

Since I became a merchant's wife,

I've in his absence passed my life.

A sailor comes home with the tide;

I should have been a sailor's bride.

LI DUAN

A ZITHERIST

How clear the golden zither rings

When her fair fingers touch its strings!

To draw attention from her lord,

Now and then she strikes a discord.

MENG JIAO

SONG OF THE PARTING SON

From the threads a mother's hand weaves
A gown for parting son is made,
Sewn stitch by stitch before he leaves
For fear his return be delayed,
Such kindness as young grass receives
From the warm sun can be repaid?

LEAVE ME NOT

I hold your robe lest you should go.
Where are you going, dear, today?
Your late return brings me less woe
Than your heart being stolen away.

SUCCESSFUL AT THE CIVIL SERVICE EXAM

Gone are all my past woes! What more have I to say?
My body and my mind enjoy their fill today.
Successful, faster runs my horse in vernal breeze,
I've seen within one day all flowers on the trees.

Rong Yu

LEAVING THE LAKESIDE PAVILION WHILE MOVING HOUSE

I love the lakeside pavilion in vernal breeze;

My sleeves are twined by twigs of weeping willow trees.

The orioles there nesting seem to know my heart;

They warble "Forget me not" songs before I part.

Yong Yuzhi

TO THE RIVERSIDE WILLOW

Your long, long branches wave by riverside,

Your green, green leaves like wreaths of smoke afloat.

"Make ropes unbreakable of them," she sighed,

"To tie up my beloved one's parting boat!"

Han Yu

To a Disgraced Official on Moon Festival

Fine clouds uprolled, the River of Stars disappears;

Moonbeams flow in waves when wind blows clouds off the spheres.

No sound nor shade on still water and level sand,

I ask you to drink and sing with wine cup in hand.

But bitter is your voice, melancholy your strain;

Before you end your song, my tears fall down like rain.

"Lake Dongting meets the sky and nine peaks tower high;

Dragons and crocodiles fly; apes and foxes cry.

At a nine-to-one risk of death I reached my post;

As if hidden from woe, in loneliness I'm lost.

I fear poison in food and snakes under my bed;

Putrid air from the lake and musty odor spread.

The county's heavy drumbeats announced yesterday

The new emperor's reign with a brilliant array.

Pardon ran thousands of miles a day out of breath;

The edict e'en commutes the punishment of death.

The exiled are recalled to the imperial town;

Those who prove guiltless may come back to serve the crown.

My name was sent in but I was given no grace,

So I'm only transferred to this primitive place.

My rank is very low and what can I tell you?

When anything goes wrong, punishment is my due.

Most of the exiled are now on their homeward way;

The road to Heaven's full of risks. What can I say?"

Please stop your song and listen to that of my mind!

Do you think my song is of a different kind?

Tonight of all the year is the brightest moonshine.

To propose is human but to dispose divine.

What shall we do if we don't drink when we have wine?

WRITTEN FOR MY GRANDNEPHEW AT THE BLUE PASS

To the Celestial Court a proposal was made,

And I am banished eight thousand miles away.

To undo the misdeeds I would have given aid.

Dare I have spared myself with powers in decay?

The Ridge veiled in barred clouds, where can my home be seen?

The Blue Pass clad in snow, my horse won't forward go.

You have come from afar and I know what you mean:

Not to leave my bones there where misty waters flow.

EARLY SPRING WRITTEN FOR SECRETARY ZHANG JI

The royal streets are moistened by a creamlike rain;

Green grass can be perceived afar but not near by.

It's the best time of a year that spring tries in vain

With the capital veiled in willows to outvie.

ZHANG JI

REPLY OF A CHASTE WIFE

You know I love my husband best,

Yet you send me two bright pearls still.

I hang them within my red silk vest,

So grateful I'm for your good will.

You see my house o'erlooks the garden and

My husband guards the palace, halberd in hand.

I know your heart as noble as the sun in the skies,

But I have sworn to serve my husband all my life.

With your twin pearls I send back two tears from my eyes.

Why did we not meet before I was made a wife?

WANG JIAN

WAITING FOR HER HUSBAND

Waiting for him alone

Where the river goes by,

She turns into a stone

Gazing with longing eye.

Atop the hill from day to day come wind and rain;

The stone should speak to see her husband come again.

A BRIDE

Married three days, I go shy-faced
To cook a soup with hands still fair.
To meet my mother in-law's taste,
I send to her daughter the first share.

ZHANG ZHONGSU

IN REVERIE

By city wall wave willows slender
And roadside mulberry leaves tender.
She gathers not, basket in hand,
Still dreaming of the far-off land.

THE PAVILION OF SWALLOWS

I

Upstairs the dying lamp flickers with morning frost;
The lonely widow rises from her nuptial bed.
Sleepless the whole night long, in mournful thoughts she's lost;
The night seems endless as the boundless sky o'erhead,

II

The pines before his grave are shrouded in sad smoke;
In the Swallows' Pavilion pensive she appears.
Her songs are hushed for buried are his sword and cloak;
Her dancing dress has lost its perfume for ten years.

III

She's seen wild geese from her lord's grave on backward way,
And now she sees the swallows come with spring again.
On flute and zither she is in no mood to play;
Buried in spider's webs and dusty they remain.

LIU YUXI

REPLY TO BAI JUYI WHOM I MEET FOR THE FIRST TIME AT A BANQUET IN YANGZHOU

O western mountains and southern streams desolate,

Where I, an exile, lived for twenty years and three!

To mourn for my departed friends I come too late;

In my native land I look like human debris.

Hundreds of sails pass by the side of sunken ship;

Thousands of flowers bloom ahead of injured tree.

Today I hear you chant the praise of comradeship;

I wish this cup of wine might well inspirit me.

THE AUTUMN BREEZE

O from where comes the autumn breeze?

It sends wild geese off sad and drear.

At dawn it enters courtyard trees;

The lonely man's the first to hear.

BAMBOO BRANCH SONGS

I

Between the green willows the river flows along;

My dear one in a boat is heard to sing a song.

The west is veiled in rain, the east enjoys sunshine;

My dear one is as deep in love as day is fine.

II

The mountain's red with peach blossoms above;

The shore is washed by spring water below.

Red blossoms fade fast as my gallant's love;

The river like my sorrow will e'er flow.

IX

The mountainside peach and plum trees blossom in tiers;

Smoke rising from the roofs amid clouds disappears.

Silver-and gold-adorned women draw water and

Men in straw hats with swords till the ash-manured land.

THE TOWN OF STONE

The changeless hills round ancient capital still stand;
Waves beating on ruined walls, unheeded, roll away.
The moon that shone by riverside on flourished land
Still shines at dead of night o'er ruined town today.

THE STREET OF MANSIONS

Beside the Bridge of Birds rank grasses overgrow;
O'er the Street of Mansions the setting sun hangs low.
Swallows that skimmed by painted eaves in bygone days
Are dipping now among the humble homes' doorways.

A SONG OF SPRING IN REPLY TO BAI JUYI

She comes downstairs in new dress that becomes her face;
When locked up, e'en spring looks sad in this lonely place.
She counts up flowers in midcourt while passing by;
On her hairpin of jade alights a dragonfly.

LAKE DONCTING VIEWED FROM AFAR

The autumn moon dissolve in soft light of the lake,
Unruffled surface like unpolished mirror bright.
Afar, the isle' mid clear water without a break
Looks like a spiral shell in a plate silver-white.

DRINKING BEFORE PEONIES IN BLOOM

Today I'll drink with blooms before.
Don't mind if I drink two cups more.
I am afraid lest to be told,
"Our bloom is not for you the old!"

THE WILLOWS

Thousands of willows see the winding river flow
Beneath the wooden bridge of twenty years ago,
On which my beauty parted with me and went away.
How I regret no news of her comes e'en today!

BAI JUYI

BUYING FLOWERS

The capital's in parting spring,

Steeds run and neigh and cab bells ring.

Peonies are at their best hours

And people rush to buy the flowers.

They do not care about the price,

Just count and buy those which seem nice.

For hundred blossoms dazzling red,

Twenty-five rolls of silk they spread.

Sheltered above by curtains wide,

Protected with fences by the side,

Roots sealed with mud, with water sprayed,

Removed, their beauty does not fade.

Accustomed to this way for long,

No family e'er thinks it wrong.

What's the old peasant doing there?

Why should he come to Flower Fair?

Head bowed, he utters sigh on sigh

And nobody understands why.

A bunch of deep-red peonies

Costs taxes of ten families.

THE WHITE-HAIRED PALACE MAID

The Shangyang Palace maid,

Her hair grows white, her rosy cheeks grow dark and fade.

The palace gate is guarded by eunuchs in green.

How many springs have passed, immured as she has been!

She was first chosen for the imperial household

At the age of sixteen; now she's sixty years old.

The hundred beauties brought in with her have all gone,

Flickering out through long years, leaving her alone.

She swallowed grief when she left home in days gone by,

Helped into the cab, she was forbidden to cry.

Once in the palace, she'd be favored, it was said;

Her face was fair as lotus, her bosom like jade.

But to the emperor she could never come nigh,

For Lady Yang had cast on her a jealous eye.

She was consigned to Shangyang Palace full of gloom,

To pass her lonely days and nights in a bare room.

In empty chamber long seemed each autumnal night; Sleepless

in bed, it seemed she'd never see daylight.

Dim, dim the lamplight throws her shadow on the walls;

Shower by shower on her window chill rain falls.

Spring days drag slow;

She sits alone to see light won't be dim and low.

She's tired to hear the palace orioles sing and sing,

Too old to envy pairs of swallows on the wing.

Silent, she sees the birds appear and disappear,

And counts nor springs nor autumns coming year by year.

Watching the moon o'er palace again and again,

Four hundred times and more she's seen it wax and wane.

Today the oldest honorable maid of all,

She is entitled Secretary of Palace Hall.

Her gown is tightly fitted, her shoes like pointed prows;

With dark green pencil she draws long, long slender brows.

Seeing her, outsiders would even laugh with tears;

Her old-fashioned dress has been out of date for years.

Oh, Shangyang maid, to suffer is her fate, all told;

She suffered while still young; she suffers now she's old.

Do you not know a satire spread in days gone by?

Today for white-haired Shangyang Palace maid we'll sigh.

THE OLD CHARCOAL SELLER

What does the old man fare?

He cuts the wood in southern hill and fires his ware,

His face is grimed with smoke and streaked with ash and dust,

His temples grizzled and his fingers all turned black.

The money earned by selling charcoal is not just

Enough for food for his mouth and clothing for his back.

Though his coat is thin, he hopes winter will set in,

For cold weather will keep up the charcoal's good price.

At night a foot of snow falls outside city walls;

At dawn his charcoal cart crushes ruts in the ice.

The sun is high, the ox tired out and hungry he;

Outside the southern gate in snow and slush they rest.

Two riders canter up, Alas! who can they be?

Two palace heralds in the yellow jackets dressed.

Decree in hand, which is imperial order, one says;

They turn the cart about and at the ox they shout.

A cartload of charcoal a thousand catties weighs;

They drive the cart away. What dare the old man say?

Ten feet of silk and twenty feet of gauze deep red—

That is the payment they fasten to the ox's head.

THE EVERLASTING REGRET

The beauty-loving monarch longed year after year

To find a beautiful lady without a peer.

A maiden of the Yangs to womanhood just grown,

In inner chambers bred, to the world was unknown.

Endowed with natural beauty too hard to hide,

She was chosen one day to be the monarch's bride.

Turning her head, she smiled so sweet and full of grace

That she outshone in six palaces the fairest face.

She bathed in glassy water of warm-fountain Pool,

Which laved and smoothed her creamy skin when spring was cool.

Without her maids' support, she was too tired to move,

And this was when she first received the monarch's love.

Flower-like face and cloud-like hair, golden-headdressed,

In lotus-adorned curtain she spent the night blessed.

She slept till the sun rose high for the blessed night was short,

From then on the monarch held no longer morning court.

In revels as in feasts she shared her lord's delight,

His companion on trips and his mistress at night.

In inner palace dwelt three thousand ladies fair;

On her alone was lavished royal love and care.

Her beauty served the night when dressed up in Golden Bower;

She was drunk with wine and spring at banquet in Jade Tower.

Her sisters and brothers all received rank and fief

And honors showered on her household, to the grief

Of fathers and mothers who would rather give birth

To a fair maiden than to any son on earth.

The lofty palace towered high into the cloud;

With divine music borne on the breeze, the air was loud.

Seeing slow dance and hearing fluted or stringed song,

The emperor was never tired the whole day long.

But rebels beat their war drums, making the earth quake

And "Song of Rainbow Skirt and Coat of Feathers" break.

A cloud of dust was raised o'er city walls nine-fold;

Thousands of chariots and horsemen southwestward rolled.

Imperial flags moved slowly now and halted then,

And thirty miles from Western Gate they stopped again.

Six armies — what could be done? — would not march with speed

Unless fair Lady Yang be killed before the steed.

None would pick up her hairpin fallen on the ground

Nor golden bird nor comb with which her head was crowned.

The monarch could not save her and hid his face in fear;

Turning his head, he saw her blood mix with his tear.

The yellow dust widespread, the wind blew desolate;

A serpentine plank path led to cloud-capped Sword Gate.

Below the Eyebrows Mountains wayfarers were few;

In fading sunlight royal standards lost their hue.

On Western water blue and Western mountains green

The monarch's heart was daily gnawed by sorrow keen.

The moon viewed from his tent shed a soul-searing light;

The bells heard in night rain made a heart-rending sound.

Suddenly turned the tide. Returning from his flight,

The monarch could not tear himself away from the ground

Where 'mid the clods beneath the Slope he couldn't forget

The fair-faced Lady Yang who was unfairly slain.

He looked at his courtiers, with tears his robe was wet;

They rode east to the capital but with loose rein.

Come back, he found her pond and garden in old place,

With lotus in the lake and willows by the hall.

Willow leaves like her brows and lotus like her face,

At the sight of all these, how could his tears not fall.

Or when in vernal breeze were peach and plum full-blown
Or when in autumn rain parasol leaves were shed?
In Western as in Southern Court was grass o'ergrown;
With fallen leaves unswept the marble steps turned red.
Actors, although still young, began to have hair grey;
Eunuchs and waiting maids looked old in palace deep.
Fireflies flitting the hall, mutely he pined away;
The lonely lampwick burned out, still he could not sleep.
Slowly beat drums and rang bells, night began to grow long;
Bright shone the Starry Stream, daybreak seemed to come late.
The love-bird tiles grew chilly with hoar frost so strong;
His kingfisher quilt was cold, not shared by a mate.
One long, long year the dead with the living was parted;
Her soul came not in dreams to see the broken-hearted,
A taoist sorcerer came to the palace door,
Skilled to summon the spirits from the other shore.
Moved by the monarch's yearning for the departed fair,
He was ordered to seek for her everywhere.
Borne on the air, like flash of lightning he flew;
In heaven and on earth he searched through and through.

Up to the azure vault and down to deepest place,

Nor above nor below could he e'er find her trace.

He learned that on the sea were fairy mountains proud

Which now appeared now disappeared amid the cloud

Of rainbow colors, where rose magnificent bowers

And dwelt so many fairies as graceful as flowers.

Among them was a queen whose name was Ever True;

Her snow-white skin and sweet face might afford a clue.

Knocking at western gate of palace hall, he bade

The fair porter to inform the queen's waiting maid.

When she heard that there came the monarch's embassy,

The queen was startled out of dreams in her canopy.

Pushing aside the pillow, she rose and got dressed,

Passing through silver screen and pearl shade to meet the guest.

Her cloud-like hair awry, not full awake at all,

Her flowery cap slanted, she came into the hall.

The wind blew up her fairy sleeves and made them float

As if she danced still "Rainbow Skirt and Feathered Coat."

Her jade-white face crisscrossed with tears in lonely world Like

a spray of pear blossoms in spring rain impearled.

She bade him thank her lord, lovesick and broken-hearted;

They knew nothing of each other after they parted.

Love and happiness long ended within palace walls;

Days and nights appeared long in the Fairyland halls.

Turning her head and fixing on the earth her gaze,

She found no capital 'mid clouds of dust and haze.

To show her love was deep, she took out keepsakes old

For him to carry back, hairpin and case of gold.

Keeping one side of the case and one wing of the pin,

She sent to her lord the other half of the twin.

"If our two hearts as firm as the gold should remain,

In heaven or on earth some time we'll meet again."

At parting, she confided to the messenger

A secret vow known only to her lord and her.

On seventh day of seventh moon when none was near,

At midnight in Long Long-life Hall he whispered in her ear:

"On high, we'd be two birds flying wing to wing;

On earth, two trees with branches twined from spring to spring."

The boundless sky and endless earth may pass away,

But this vow unfulfilled will be regretted for aye.

Song of a Pipa Player

One night by riverside I bade a friend goodbye;

In maple leaves and rushes autumn seemed to sigh.

My friend and I dismounted and came into the boat;

We wished to drink but there was no music afloat.

Without flute songs we drank our cups with heavy heart;

The moonbeams blent with water when we were to part.

Suddenly o'er the stream we heard a pipa sound;

I forgot to go home and the guest stood spell-bound.

We followed where the music led to find the player,

But heard the pipa stop and no music in the air.

We moved our boat towards the one whence came the strain,

Brought back the lamp, asked for more wine and drank again.

Repeatedly we called for the fair player till

She came, her face half hidden behind a pipa still.

She turned the pegs and tested twice or thrice each string;

Before a tune was played we heard her feelings sing.

Each string she plucked, each note she struck with pathos strong,

All seemed to say she'd missed her dreams all her life long.

Head bent, she played with unpremeditated art

On and on to pour out her overflowing heart.

She lightly plucked, slowly stroked and twanged loud

The song of "Green Waist" after that of "Rainbow Cloud."

The thick strings loudly thrummed like the pettering rain;

The fine strings softly tinkled in a murmuring strain.

When mingling loud and soft notes were together played,

You heard large and small pearls cascade on plate of jade.

Now you heard orioles warble in flowery land,

Then a sobbing stream run along a beach of sand.

But the stream seemed so cold as to tighten the string;

From tightenied strings no more sound could be heard to sing.

Still we heard hidden grief and vague regret concealed;

Then music expressed far less than silence revealed.

Suddenly we heard water burst a silver jar,

And the clash of spears and sabres come from afar.

She made a central sweep when the music was ending;

The four strings made one sound, as of silk one was rending.

Silence reigned left and right of the boat, east and west;

We saw but autumn moon white in the river's breast.

She slid the plectrum pensively between the strings,

Smoothed out her dress and rose with a composed mien.

"I spent," she said, "in the capital my early springs,

Where at the foot of Mount of Toads my home had been.

At thirteen I learned on the pipa how to play,

And my name was among the primas of the day.

I won my master's admiration for my skill

My beauty was envied by songstresses fair still.

The gallant young men vied to shower gifts on me;

One tune played, countless silk rolls were given with glee.

Beating time, I let silver comb and pin drop down,

And spilt-out wine oft stained my blood-red silken gown.

From year to year I laughed my joyous life away

On moonlit autumn night as windy vernal day.

My younger brother left for war, and died my maid;

Days passed, nights came, and my beauty began to fade.

Fewer and fewer were cabs and steeds at my door;

I married a smug merchant when my prime was o'er.

The merchant cared for money much more than for me;

One month ago he went away to purchase tea,

Leaving his lonely wife alone in empty boat;

Shrouded in moonlight, on the cold river I float.

Deep in the night I dreamed of happy bygone years,

And woke to find my rouged face crisscrossed with tears."

Listening to her sad music, I sighed with pain;

Hearing her story, I sighed again and again.

"Both of us in misfortune go from shore to shore.

Meeting now, need we have known each other before?

I was banished from the capital last year

To live degraded and ill in this city here.

The city's too remote to know melodious song,

So I have never heard music all the year long.

I dwell by riverbank on a low and damp ground

In a house with wild reeds and stunted bamboos around.

What is here to be heard from daybreak till nightfall

But gibbon's cry and cuckoo's homeward-going call?

By blooming riverside and under autumn moon

I've often taken wine up and drunk it alone.

Though I have mountain songs and village pipes to hear,

Yet they are crude and strident and grate on the ear.

Listening to you playing on pipa tonight,

With your music divine e'en my hearing seems bright.

Will you sit down and play for us a tune once more?

I'll write for you an ode to the pipa I adore."

Touched by what I said, the player stood for long,

Then sat down, tore at strings and played another song.

So sad, so drear, so different, it moved us deep;

Those who heard it hid the face and began to weep.

Of all the company at table who wept most?

It was none other than the exiled blue-robed host.

A FLOWER IN THE HAZE

In bloom, she's not a flower;

Hazy, she's not a haze.

She comes at midnight hour;

She goes with starry rays.

She comes like vernal dreams that cannot stay;

She goes like morning clouds that melt away.

GRASS ON THE ANCIENT PLAIN — FAREWELL TO A FRIEND

Wild grasses spread o'er ancient plain;

With spring and fall they come and go.

Fire tries to burn them up in vain;

They rise again when spring winds blow.

Their fragrance overruns the way;

Their green invades the ruined town.

To see my friend going away,

My sorrow grows like grass o'ergrown.

THE LAST LOOK ON THE PEONIES AT NIGHT

I'm saddened by the courtyard peonies brilliant red;

At dusk only two of them are left on their bed.

I am afraid they can't survive the morning blast;

By lantern light I take a look, the long, long last.

THE PAVILION OF SWALLOWS
AFTER ZHANG ZHONGSU'S POEMS, USING THE SAME RHYME SCHEME

I

Her room is drowned in moonlight and the screen in frost;
The quilt grows cold with dying lamp, she makes the bed.
The moonlit night in which Swallows' Pavilion's lost,
Since autumn came, lengthens for one who mourns the dead.

II

Her silken dress with golden flowers fades like smoke;
She tries to put it on, but soon she melts in tears.
Since she no longer danced to the air of "Rainbow Cloak,"
It has been stored up in the chest for ten long years.

III

Some friends coming back from ancient capital say
They've visited the grave of her dear lord again.
The graveyard poplar white grows high as pillar gray.
How can her rosy face still beautiful remain?

PEACH BLOSSOMS IN THE TEMPLE OF GREAT FOREST

All flowers in late spring have fallen far and wide,

But peach blossoms are full-blown on the mountainside.

I oft regret spring's gone without leaving its trace;

I do not know it's come up to adorn this place.

AN INVITATION

My new brew gives green glow;

My red clay stove flames up.

At dusk it threatens snow.

Won't you come for a cup?

THE DESERTED

Her kerchief soaked with tears, she cannot fall asleep,

But overhears band music waft when night is deep.

Her rosy face outlasts the favor of the king;

She leans on her perfumed bed till morning birds sing.

SUNSET AND MOONRISE ON THE RIVER

The departing sunbeams pave a way on the river;

Half of its waves turn red and the other half shiver.

How I love the third night of the ninth moon aglow!

The dewdrops look like pearls; the crescent like a bow.

ON LAKE QIANTANG IN SPRING

West of Pavilion Jia and north of Lonely Hill,

Water brims level with the bank and clouds hang low.

Disputing for sunny trees, early orioles trill;

Pecking vernal mud in, young swallows come and go.

A riot of blooms begin to dazzle the eye;

Amid short grass the horse hoofs can barely be seen.

I love best the east of the lake under the sky:

The bank paved with white sand is shaded by willows green.

WHITE CLOUD FOUNTAIN

Behold the White Cloud Fountain on the Sky-blue Mountain!

White clouds enjoy free pleasure; water enjoys leisure.

Why should the torrent dash down from the mountain high,

And overflow the human world with waves far and nigh?

THE RED COCKATOO

Annam has sent us from afar a red cockatoo;

Colored like the peach blossom, it speaks as men do.

But it is shut up in a cage with bar on bar

Just as the learned or eloquent scholars are.

DEPRESSION

Hugging my pillow, what to say?

My empty room's in silence deep.

Who knows I lie in bed all day,

Not ill and not even asleep?

ILLNESS

My bosom friends need not worry too much for me;
Somehow I'll take a walk if from illness I'm free.
When I want to go far, I need not use my feet;
Sedan by land and boat on water are as fleet.

YANG SHI'E

MOUNTING THE TOWER

Sparse scholar-trees and willows gird the city walls;
Rain's streamed downhill since last night as a river bawls.
When autumn gale blows, nor horse nor cart are in sight.
How can I not be homesick alone on the height!

Liu Zao

FARTHER NORTH

Ten long, long winters in northern town I did stay;

My heart cried out for my southern home night and day.

Now as I cross the river, farther north I roam;

My heart cries out for northern town as for my home.

Liu Zongyuan

TO FOUR FRIENDS IN EXILE

From the high tower I see the wilderness looms;

My sad thoughts mingle with the boundless sea and sky.

A sudden gale disturbs the pool with lotus blooms;

A slanting rain attacks the wall where vines climb high.

Dense trees on mountain ridge shut out the distant view;

The river meanders like tortuous bowels long.

Coming among barbarians together with you,

I've not received your message brought by wild geese's song.

FISHING IN SNOW

From hill to hill no bird in flight;

From path to path no man in sight.

A lonely fisherman afloat

Is fishing snow in lonely boat.

A FISHERMAN

Under western cliff a fisherman passed the night;

At dawn he made bamboo fire to boil water clean.

Mist cleared off at sunrise but there's no man in sight;

Only the fisherman's song turns hill and rill green.

He goes down mid-stream and turns to look on the sky.

What does he see but clouds freely wafting on high?

DRINKING

I fill my cup with drink divine;
It is another boring day.
First let me drink to Lord of Wine,
Who helps to drive the blues away.
One draught and different I feel;
At once the world revives anew.
See what the hidden hills reveal!
The river takes on warming hue.
Exuberant at southern gate,
Leafy trees look like paradise.
With shade their roots are saturate;
All night you hear silent advice.
Drink your fill and gargle your mouth!
Drunk, you may lie on fragrant grass.
O rich revelers north and south!
What have you in your cups, alas!

Cui Hu

Written in a Village South of the Capital

In this house on this day last year, a pink face vied
In beauty with the pink peach blossoms side by side.
I do not know today where the pink face has gone;
In vernal breeze still smile pink peach blossoms full-blown.

Yuan Zhen

To My Deceased Wife

I

Youngest daughter of your family, loved the best,
Unluckily you married into my poor household.
To patch my clothes you would search your dowry chest;
Coaxed to buy me wine you'd pledge a hairpin of gold.
For fuel you'd burn dry leaves from old locust tree;
For meals we were glad to eat but wild herbs and rice.
More than a hundred thousand coins are now paid me,
But I can bring you only temple sacrifice.

II

"What if one of us should die?" we said for fun one day;
But now it has come true and passed before my eyes.
I can't bear to see your clothes and give them away;
I seal your embroidery lest it should draw my sighs.
Remembering your kindness, I'm kind to our maids;
Dreaming of your bounty, I give bounties as before.
I know there is no mortal but returns to the shades,
But a poor couple like us have more to deplore.

III

Sitting idle, I grieve for myself as for you.
How many days are left of my declining years?
Another childless man fared better than I do;
Another widower lavished vain verse and tears.
Could I await a better fate than our same tomb?
Could you be born again and again be my wife?
With eyes unclosed all night long I'll be in the gloom
To repay you for your unknit brows in your life.

AT AN OLD PALACE

Deserted now imperial bowers,
For whom still redden palace flowers?
A white-haired chambermaid at leisure
Tells of the late emperor's pleasure.

CHRYSANTHEMUMS

Around the cottage like Tao's autumn flowers grow;
Along the hedge I stroll until the sun slants low.
Not that I favor partially the chrysanthemum,
But it is the last flower after which none will bloom.

THINKING OF MY DEAR DEPARTED

No water's wide enough when you have crossed the sea;

No cloud is beautiful but that which crowns the peak.

I pass by flowers which fail to attract poor me

Half for your sake and half for Taoism I seek.

JIA DAO

A SWORDSMAN

I've sharpened my sword for ten years;

I do not know if it will pierce.

I show its blade to you today.

O who has any grievance? Say!

MY LORD'S GARDEN

A thousand homes shattered, a garden is laid out;

Roses grow everywhere, but no fruit-bearing trees.

When the autumn wind blows and roses fall about,

Can you sit in the thorn-choked pavilion with ease?

FOR AN ABSENT RECLUSE

I ask your lad 'neath a pine tree.
"My master's gone for herbs," says he.
You hide amid the mountains proud,
I know not where deep in the cloud.

LI SHEN

THE PEASANTS

I

Each seed that's sown in spring
Will make autumn yields high.
What will fertile fields bring?
Of hunger peasants die.

II

At noon they weed with hoes;
Their sweat drips on the soil.
Each bowl of rice, who knows?
Is the fruit of hard toil.

Xue Tao

Spring View

I

Blooming flowers not together enjoyed,

At their fall we're not together annoyed.

Don't ask me why I'm lovesick, sad and drear

To see flowers appear and disappear!

II

I braid two blades of grass into one heart

And send it to my lover far apart.

I've just got rid of my old vernal sorrow.

Who knows birds sing again a mournful morrow!

III

Like bloom in wind I'm growing old;

Our happy date can't be foretold.

When our hearts are not one, alas!

What's the use of love-knot in grass?

IV

How can I bear a lovesick heart

From blooming flowers kept apart?

Does spring wind know my face appears

Before the mirror wet with tears?

TO THE BAMBOO AFTER RAIN

When spring rain falls on southern roof,

Who remembers you are cold-proof?

From the lush plants you stand apart;

Alone you keep your modest heart.

The drunken sages are your compeers;

Your stems are stained with royal tears.

We know your worth in winter cold;

E'ergreen and strong, you won't grow old.

SENDING OLD POEMS TO YUAN ZHEN

Each poet or poetess has his style or her own;

I know mine is subtle and delicate alone.

I sing of moonlit flowers in melancholy strain;

I write of weeping willows shedding tears in rain.

Like hidden emerald I'm ever kept apart;

On my self-made rosy leaf I pour out my heart.

Growing too old to sort my poems one by one,

I send you these old ones you may show to your son.

ZHANG HU

THE SWAN SONG

Homesick a thousand miles away,
Shut in deep palace twenty years,
Singing the dying swan's sweet lay,
O how can she hold back her tears!

A PALACE MAID

The moon cast shadows of a tree on palace door;
Her longing eyes saw a nest of birds and no more.
Drawing her jade hairpin near a candle she came
To save a moth by brushing aside the red flame.

LONG-LIFE TERRACE

The Duchess of Guo State had won imperial grace;
At dawn she rode through palace gates with dignity.
Disdainful of the paint which might have marred her face,
With lightly touched-up brows she met His Majesty.

AT JINLING FERRY HEAD

In little hut at ferry head where people part,
A lonely traveler can't but feel sad at heart.
The moon slants o'er the ebbing river in the gloom,
And on the islet two or three weak flickers loom.

Li She

LODGING AGAIN AT THE SOUTHERN PASS

Leaving the capital with a long way to go,
I stay at Southern Pass where hills rise high and low.
The city gate cannot lock in the cold brook's song;
It murmurs about my parting grief all night long.

Cui Jiao

TO THE MAID OF MY AUNT

Even sons of prince and lord try to find thy trace;
Thy scarf is wet with pearl-like tears dropped from thy face.
The mansion where thou enter is deep as the sea;
Thy master from now on is a stranger to thee.

LI HE

DEFENSE OF THE WILD GEESE GATE

Dark clouds threaten the town, its walls risk to be worn;

Defenders' sunlit armour glitters like scales bright.

The sky in autumn hue is loud with blowing horn;

The rouge-congealed frontier dissolves in purple night.

Our half-unfurled red flags come to shivering stream;

Laden with heavy frost, cold drumbeats can't rise high.

We'd do our best to realize our lord's golden dream,

Jade-dragon sword in hand, we're not afraid to die.

TOMB OF SU, YOUNG BEAUTY

On lonely orchid dew

Looks like tear in your eye.

Whose heart is one with you?

Flowers in mist would cry.

Carpet-like grass would sing

Canopy-like pine trees.

Ripples as pendants ring;

Your robe wafts in the breeze.

Your cab of painted sheen

Waits long for happy night.

Your chilly candle green

Kindles flames and sheds light

On your west tomb in vain,

For wind has changed to rain.

DREAMING OF THE SKY

The lunar toad's and rabbit's tears wash the cold sky;

Half-open bowers in the cloud shed slanting ray.

Jade wheels roll over dew and moisten light on high;

The Beauty of the Moon comes down her laurel way.

Dust turns to water pure as in a fairy star;

A thousand years have changed like horses on the run.

I see nine wreaths of smoke rise from the land afar,

And the sea pours into a cup under the sun.

SONG OF HEAVEN

Stars float on Heavenly River turning at night;

Clouds over silver shores mimic the rippling song.

Laurel flowers have not fallen from Lunar Height;

Fairies gather fragrance with pendants hanging long.

The princess rolls up screens to welcome dawning day;

The blue phoenix is overshadowed by the plane tree.

An immortal blows the painted flute in his way,

And calls dragons to plough mist and plant herb with glee.

In rainbow dress and lotus skirt with ribbon red,

Fairies gather spring orchids in Azure Isle.

Pointing to the charioteer of the Sun God ahead,

They find sea dust form stony mountain in a while.

A FULL SONG

The southern wind blows down hills and flat land appears;

The God of Water moves the sea from east to west.

The peach divine has turned red many thousand years;

The oldest man and witch are dead and lie in rest.

I ride a piebald horse dappled in color fine;

Willows exhale light wreaths of smoke in charming spring.

The lute-player offers a golden cup of wine.

Before my blood and spirit fuse, what can I sing?

Don't drink and sing in praise of the governor old!

A hero may not meet a connoisseur in his life.

I would like to buy silk and embroider in gold

The image of the lord who had won all in strife.

As water drips from the clock, time passes away,

Thin would become the hair of the beautiful queen.

How could a twenty-year-old man not fight his way,

When he sees autumn eyebrows change into new green?

AUTUMN COMES

The wind blows down plane leaves and moves my heart to rue;

Spinners weaving cold silk weep by flickering light.

Who will read the deep words inscribed on the bamboo

And keep worms boring powderly holes out of sight?

Such nocturnal thoughts would stretch my intestine straight,

But sweet phantom's cold tears would rain down for their peer.

Ghosts would come out of tombs to mourn the poet's fate;

Blood would turn earth to emerald from year to year.

THE EMPEROR DRINKS

The emperor rides on tiger to eight frontiers;

His sword brightens the air and greens celestial spheres.

His charioteer strikes the sun with a tinkling sound;

A peaceful world emerges out of the battleground.

Wine sprouting from dragon's head invites drinking star;

The golden pipa's night song can be heard afar.

Rain coming from the lake blows the flute for the guest;

Drunken, the moon is ordered to go east from west.

Silvery cloud on cloud brightens the jasper hall;

The gate-keeper announes first watch after nightfall.

The angry charming songstress sings in painted tower;

The rippled rosy silk exhales fragerance of flower,

The yellow-dressed dancers drink health of long, long years.

From the chandelier wreath by wreath light smoke appears;

From fair lute-player's drunken eyes stream down sad tears.

MY SOUTHERN GARDEN

I

Blooming branches and creepers spread before the eye;

Rosy flowers with maiden's cheeks in beauty vie.

At sunset fallen fragrant petals cannot please,

But wed without a go-between to vernal breeze.

V

Why does a man not join the army, sword in hand,

And pass mountains and streams to occupy the land?

If you should go up the tower scraping the sky,

You'd find no scholar could become a general high.

VI

Should I waste time to find the best words in best order

Until the waning moon looks like a jade bow?

Do you not see the war raging on northern border?

How can a poet grieve to hear autumn wind blow?

VII

The unemployed talent lived in an empty room;

The humorist made fun to lighten the deep gloom.

I'd like to buy and sharpen a sword by the stream,

And learn from Master Ape how to fulfill my dream.

VIII

Spring water rises when young swallows learn to fly;

Bees come back when they've gathered honey from the flowers.

The window screens enframe scenes far-off and near-by;

A scented hook attracts the fish where a lock towers.

THE BRONZE STATUE LEAVING HAN PALACE

In the eighth month of the year 237 the emperor of Wei sent A eunuch to bring from the west the bronze statue holding A moon-shaped plate to catch the immortal dew, erected by Emperor Wu of the Han Dynasty, and to place it in the front Court at Luoyang. Dismantled, the bronze shed tears before His departure, so I write the following song.

The emperor was gone just like his autumn breeze;
At night his steed would neigh, at dawn no trace was seen.
By painted rails fragrance still wafts o'er laurel trees,
His thirty palaces o'ergrown with mosses green.
Wei eunuch drove a dray to go a long, long way;
In Eastern Pass the sour wind stung the bronze's eyes.
Only the moon of yore saw him leave palace door;
Thinking of his dear lord, he shed tears and heaved sighs.
Withered orchids would say, "Farewell and go your way!"
Heaven would have grown old if it could feel as man.
He went with moon-shaped plate 'neath the moon desolate;
The waves unheard, far from the town the horses ran.

HORSE POEMS (FOUR SELECTIONS)

I

A string of coins on the horse's back, noble and proud,
His hoofs silver-white as though born to trot in cloud.
But where are whip of gold and saddle cloth of brocade?
The cloth is not yet woven and whip not yet made.

IV

This is no ordinary steed
But an incarnate star indeed.
When I tap his bony frame, what's found?
I seem to hear metallic sound.

V

The desert sands look white as snow;
The crescent moon hangs like a bow.
When would the steed in golden gear
Gallop all night through autumn clear?

XXIII

"I'll have elixir," Emperor Wu says,
And heaps of gold go up in purple haze.
All steeds in royal stable, ah, must die,
For none of them can run up to the sky.

SONG OF THE HOLY STRINGS

East hills are darkened when on west hills sinks the sun;

The whirlwind blows clouds away on which horses run.

The painted lute and pipe play music high and low;

The witch in rustling flowered skirt comes in sunset glow.

Laurel leaves and seeds are blown down by autumn breath;

Blue racoons weep over the fox frozen to death.

Dragons with golden tails are painted on the wall,

But God of Rain drives them to autumn waterfall.

The hundred-year-old owl transformed into a pest

Bursts in laughter to see green flames rise from its nest.

LET US DRINK

From crystal cup

Amber-red wine

Drips drop by drop like crimson pearls divine.

Let's drink it up

With dragon boiled and roasted phoenix green,

Sweetened by scented breeze from silken screen!

Blow the dragon-like flute;

Beat drums of crocodile skin!

Songstress will not be mute;

Slender waists dance, though thin.

Now spring will end and the sun will be sunken;

Peach blossoms fall in a riot of petals red.

Let us drink all the day long till we're drunken!

The poet fond of wine could not drink when he's dead.

WATCHMAN'S DRUMBEAT ON OFFICIAL STREET

At dawn my booming drumbeat hastens circling sun;

At dusk it calls forth the silver moon to rise and run.

Imperial willows cast shadow on palace screen;

In cypress-shaded tomb lie fragrant bones of the queen.

I pound a thousand years to pieces with sticks strong.

Coul the first or martial emperor live as long?

Your hair may turn from black to white as reeds in bloom;

I'll guard the capital with South Mountains in gloom.

Even if immortals are buried in the sky,

My drum will boom with waterclock and never die.

Xu Hun

GAZING AFAR IN THE EVENING FROM THE WEST TOWER OF XIANYANG

On city wall I see grief spread for miles and miles

O'er reeds and willow trees as planted on flats and isles.

The sun beneath the cloud sinks o'er waterside bower;

The wind before the storm fills the mountainside tower.

In the wasted Qin garden only birds fly still;

'Mid yellow leaves in Han palace cicadas shrill.

O wayfarer, don't ask about the days gone by!

Coming from east, I hear only the river sigh.

FRONTIER SONG

In snow our men did fight;

Half of them died at night.

But letters came next day:

Winter clothes on the way.

PARTING AT RIVERSIDE TOWER

After the farewell song your boat departs by day
On rapid stream between green mountains and red leaves.
When I'm sober from wine at dusk, you're far away;
When I go down, a skyful of wind and rain grieves.

XU NING

TO ONE IN YANGZHOU

Your bashful face could hardly bear the weight of tears;
Your long, long brows would easily feel sorrow nears.
Of all the moonlit nights on earth when people part,
Two-thirds shed light upon Yangzhou with broken heart.

Du Mu

THE SUMMER PALACE

Viewed from afar, the hill's paved with brocades in piles;
The palace doors on hilltops opened one by one.
A steed which raised red dust won the fair mistress' smiles.
How many steeds which brought her fruit died on the run!

A POET'S GRAVEYARD

Who would thyme with the poet singing from the heart?
He is buried amid weed and moss, far apart.
At the foot of the hill I try to seek his trace
Only to find his rippling voice and moonlit lace.

WRITTEN AT PLEASURE SEEKING PLAIN BEFORE LEAVING FOR THE SOUTHERN SEASIDE TOWN

Useless when unemployed under a peaceful reign,

I love a lonely cloud and a monk's tranquillity.

With flags and banners I'd leave for the seaside plain,

How could I leave the great tomb of His Majesty!

THE WEST BAMBOO TEMPLE AT YANGZHOU

A cicada's loud after rain;

Pine trees of sad autumn complain.

Green moss spreads o'er steps at the gate;

White birds intend to linger late.

Out of deep woods evening mist grows;

Down the tower the setting sun goes.

From West Bamboo Road further down,

You'll hear songs of Riverside Town.

SPRING ON THE SOUTHERN RIVERSHORE

Orioles sing for miles 'mid red blooms and green trees;

By hills and rills wineshop streamers wave in the breeze.

Four hundred eighty splendid temples still remain

Of Southern Dynasties in the mist and the rain.

RUINED SPLENDOR

Rank grasses grow, Six Dynasties splendor's no more;

The sky is lightly blue and clouds free as of yore.

Birds come and go into the gloom of wooded hills,

And songs and wails alike merge in murmuring rills.

Like countless window curtains falls late autumn rain;

High towers steeped in sunset, wind and flute's refrain.

O how I miss the lakeside sage of bygone days!

I see but ancient trees loom ragged in the haze.

WRITTEN FOR ZHANG HU AT NINE PEAK TOWER

How could I be free from my upsurging regret

To hear the lonely horn rise at Tower of Sunset!

Green mountains extend far as my longing for you.

When may I see the outspread fragrant grass anew?

The eye can't see the eyelash though it is nearby.

What need you seek when you find the way low and high?

No one is higher than your poetical mind;

A thousand verses leave ten thousand lords behind.

ON MOUNTAIN-CLIMBING DAY

Autumn's dissolved in waves when wild geese backward fly;

Wine cup in hand, we climb Emerald Mountain high.

It is not easy to laugh with mouth open wide;

Back, with chrysanthemums we should be beautified.

Let us drink our fill to enjoy our holiday;

Do not regret with setting sun time passed away!

Life is full of ups and downs now as long ago.

Why should we shed vain tears for the past weal and woe?

ON MY WAY TO LAKESIDE TOWN

Halfway over creekside bridge the sun's going to set;
Half a wreath of light smoke wafts amid willow trees.
How lotus leaves lean on each other with regret?
All at once they turn back against the western breeze.

SPRING ABIDES NOT

Spring days half gone to the year's end amount;
For all the other seasons do not count.
I drink to flowers loath to say adieu
And feel e'en wine would taste like winter brew.
I am distressed after the parting cup;
The broom will sweep all fallen petals up.
From year to year thus life will pass away.
O who can stop it on its eastward way!

THE RED CLIFF

We dig out broken halberds buried in the sand
And wash and rub these relics of an ancient war.
Had the east wind refused General Zhou a helping hand,
His foe'd have locked his fair wife on northern shore.

MOORED ON RIVER QINHUAI

Cold water and sand bars veiled in misty moonlight,
I moor on River Qinhuai near wineshops at night.
The songstress knows not the grief of the captive king,
By riverside she sings his song of Parting Spring.

AT PARTING

I
Not yet fourteen, she's fair and slender
Like early budding flower tender.
Though Yangzhou Road's beyond compare,
Pearly screens uprolled, none's so fair.

II

Deep, deep our love, too deep to show;

Deep, deep we drink; silent we grow.

The candle grieves to see us part:

It melts in tears with burnt-out heart.

A CONFESSION

I roved the rivers, indulged in pleasure and wine

With slender Southern girls who'd dance on palms of mine.

Having dreamed happy dreams ten years, I woke a rover

Who earned in mansions green the name of fickle lover.

GOING UP THE HILL

A slanting stony path leads far to the cold hill;

Where fleecy clouds are born, there appear cots and bowers.

I stop my cab at maple woods to gaze my fill;

Frost-bitten leaves look redder than early spring flowers.

AN AUTUMN NIGHT

Autumn has chilled the painted screen in candlelight;
A palace maid uses a fan to catch fireflies.
The steps seem steeped in water when cold grows the night;
She sits to watch two stars in love meet in the skies.

THE GOLDEN VALLEY GARDEN IN RUINS

Past splendors are dispersed and blend with fragrant dust;
Unfeelingly rivers run and grass grows in spring.
At dusk the flowers fall in the eastern wind just
Like Green Pearl tumbling down and birds mournfully sing.

THE MOURNING DAY

A drizzling rain falls like tears on the Mourning Day;
The mourner's heart is going to break on his way.
Where can a wineshop be found to drown his sad hours?
A cowherd points to a cot 'mid apricot flowers.

Yong Tao

THE BRIDGE OF LOVE'S END

Why should this bridge be called Love's End,
Since love without an end will last?
Plant willow trees for parting friend;
Your longing for him will stand fast.

Zhu Qingyu

WITHIN THE PALACE

The palace gate is closed, even flowers feel lonely;
Fair maidens side by side in shade of arbour stand.
They will complain of their lonesome palace life, only
Afraid the parrot might tell a tale secondhand.

TO AN EXAMINER ON THE EVE OF EXAMINATION

Last night red candles burned bright in the bridal room;

At dawn the bride will bow to new parents with the groom.

She whispers to him after touching up her face:

"Have I painted my brows with fashionable grace?"

WEN TINGYUN

AT THE WATERSHED

The heartless stream appears to have a heart;

It goes with me in the hills for three days long.

At watershed on mountain top we part;

All the night long it sings a farewell song.

TO SNOW IN THE THIRD MOON

In third moon you fall all the night;

You don't mean to harm flowers fair.

You fear spring will pass out of sight;

You'd accompany lonesome pear.

EARLY DEPARTURE

At dawn I rise and my cab bells begin
To ring, but in thoughts of home I am lost.
The cock crows as the moon sets o'er thatched inn;
Footprints are left on wood bridge paved with frost.
The mountain path is covered with oak leaves;
The posthouse bright with blooming orange trees.
The dream of my homeland last night still grieves:
A pool of mallards playing with wild geese.

LI SHANGYIN

THE SAD ZITHER

Why should the sad zither have fifty strings?
Each string, each strain evokes but vanished springs:
Dim morning dream to be a butterfly;
Amorous heart poured out in cuckoo's cry.
In moonlit pearls see tears in mermaid's eyes;
With sunburned mirth let blue jade vaporise.
Such feeling cannot be recalled again;
It seemed long lost e'en when it was felt then.

PASSING AGAIN THE TEMPLE OF A GODDESS

Over your door of white rock I see green moss grow;

You're banished from the paradise where you can't go.

The dreaming vernal rains with your tiles often play;

The wonder-working wind won't swell your flag all day.

There is no place to shelter fair Emerald Flower,

And Fragrant Orchid won't stay here more than an hour.

The Registrar of Jade knows you come from on high.

Let miraculous herb bring you back to the sky!

FOR AN EXILED FRIEND

Waves surge when blows the wind, clouds rooted in rocks shiver,

The mast and anchor tremble on the darkened river.

How could the northern swan fly up with broken wings?

How could the exiled poet find his Southern springs?

Who would answer the summons of the royal court?

A poet would sing freely the days long or short.

Happy to meet so far from homeland, we shed tears.

When could the phoenix fly to nine celestial spheres!

ON THE PLAIN OF TOMBS

At dusk my heart is filled with gloom;
I drive my cab to ancient tomb.
The setting sun seems so sublime,
But it is near its dying time.

THE DOWNFALL OF KINGDOM QI

I
The king loved less his kingdom than his beauty's smiles.
Could his palace not be buried in briars for miles?
His favored lady lay in bed on full display,
While the foe entered his capital in array.

II
How could a beauty's smile overshadow state affair?
The king was charmed by his lady in hunting dress.
Of his capital in danger he did not care;
He would go hunting one more round nevertheless.

WRITTEN ON A RAINY NIGHT TO MY WIFE IN THE NORTH

You ask me when I can return, but I don't know;
It rains in western hills and autumn pool o'erflow.
When can we trim by window side the candlelight
And talk about the western hills in rainy night?

WIND AND RAIN

As an unused sword I'm as drear.
Oh, when will end my roaming year!
Yellow leaves fall in winds and rains;
Green mansions play strings and sing strains.
My new friends are left in the cold;
Can I often meet my peers old?
How I long for nectar divine
To drown my lonely grief in wine!

FOR A FRIEND

We're severed long by northern cloud and western trees;
Your letter's sent to quench my thirst from far away.
Don't ask about your friend in lonely garden, please!
Just read the poet sick with rainy autumn day!

ELEGY ON LIU FEN

Closed are the palace gates of the celestial spheres;
No witch is sent down to inquire if you're right or wrong.
Spring tides have severed us since we parted in tears;
Your death turns tears to autumn rain weeping all day long.
I would turn rain drops into words to mourn for you.
Could the poet call back the soul of my compeer?
I admire you as an old friend and teacher new.
How could I weep for you in and out, far and near!

FOR DU MU

Your verse exhales spring wind and rain in tower high,
Left far behind with my short swallow wings, I sigh.
At parting spring and parting with friends old and new,
Who in the world is drowned in deeper grief than you?

WOULD DU FU NOT LEAVE THE FAREWELL FEAST?

Could we have no meeting and parting in our life?
But parting would bring grief in time of war and strife.
The peace envoy has not come back from the frontiers;
Our forts are guarded still by royal cavaliers.
The drunken in the feast talk to the sober loud,
While on the river float fleecy cloud and dark cloud.
"Won't good wine intoxicate you all your life long,
If accompanied by a beauty's sweeter song?"

THE SUI PALACE

The Palace of Purple Spring lost in rainbow cloud
Might be replaced by new one in riverside town.
Were the emperor not overthrown by the crowd,
His royal ship might sail to new sky's end unknown.
But now no fireflies overspread the withered grass;
Only dark crows perch on his weeping willow trees.
If he met underground his captive king, alas!
Could the sweet song of their palace flowers still please?

THE SECOND DAY OF THE SECOND MOON

On second day of second moon I sail on stream,

The vernal wind brings warmth and I hear flutist sing.

Red flowers have no heart and green willows no dream,

But purple butterflies and golden bees love spring.

How can I live from my homeland so far apart?

In willow camp I've done my duty for three years.

The rippling stream can't understand a roamer's heart:

The night rain dripping from old roof assails my ears.

THE PREMIER'S MILITARY STATION

Monkeys and birds have not forgot the Premier's order;

Still wind and cloud would screen and shield his ancient border.

In vain had he made prodigeous strategic plan;

At last the captive king was gone in prison van.

He had the talent of wise marshalls in their prime.

What could he do with generals lost before their time!

When people visit his temple in later days,

Their regret would outlast the song sung in his praise.

TO ONE UNNAMED

As last night twinkle stars, as last night blows the breeze

West of the painted bower, east of Cassia Hall.

Having no wings, I can't fly to you as I please;

Our hearts at one, yo ur ears can hear my inner call.

Maybe you're playing hook in palm and drinking wine

Or guessing what the cup hides under candle red.

Alas! I hear the drum call me to duties mine;

Like rootless weed to Orchid Hall I ride ahead.

THREE POEMS TO ONE UNNAMED

I

You said you'd come, but you are gone and left no trace;

I wake to hear in moonlit tower the fifth watch bell.

In dream my cry could not call you back from distant place;

In haste with ink unthickened I cannot write well.

The candlelight illuminates half our broidered bed;

The smell of musk still faintly sweetens lotus screen.

Beyond my reach the far-off fairy mountains spread,

But you're still farther off than fairy mountains green.

II

The rustling eastern wind came with a drizzle light,

And thunder faintly rolled beyond the lotus pool.

When doors were locked and incense burned, I came at night,

And went at dawn when windlass pulled up water cool.

You peeped at me first from behind a curtained bower;

I'm left at last only with a cushion of your name.

Let my desire not bloom and vie with vernal flower!

For inch by inch my heart is consumed by the flame.

IV

From where come happy flute song and lyric full of gloom?

From willowy shore and long lane where cherries bloom.

The eastern villager's poor beauty is not wed,

Though like the sun of late spring shining overhead.

The rich and noble princess is only fourteen;

Suitors on mourning day break walls and willow screen.

How could the old maid not toss in bed deep in night?

Even swallows on the beam would sigh for her plight.

THE SUI PALACE (II)

The pleasure-seeking monarch toured the South at will.
Who dare alert him in the ninth celestial sphere?
People were forced to weave brocade through the mill
But half was used as mudguard and half as sail too dear.

TO THE WILLOW

Having caressed the dancers in the vernal breeze,
You're ravished amid the merry-making trees.
How can you wait until clear autumn days are done
To shrill like poor cicadas in the setting sun?

TO ONE UNNAMED

It's difficult for us to meet and hard to part;
The east wind is too weak to revive flowers dead.
Spring silkworm till its death spins silk from lovesick heart;
Candles only when burned up have no tears to shed.
At dawn I'm grieved to think your mirrored hair turns grey;
At night you would feel cold while I croon by moonlight.
To the three fairy hills it is not a long way.
Would the blue birds oft fly to see you on the height!

GREEN RAINBOW CLOUD

Twelve balustrades wind in the town of rainbow cloud,

Where rhino and jade keep dust and cold air away.

The crane would send the fairy's love to phoenix proud,

There is no tree by the wall where no lovebirds stay.

Stars seen before the window sink deep into the night,

And bring showers for thirsting flowers by the stream.

If the pearl of the morning should be ever bright,

How could the fairy face the crystal moon in dream?

SONG OF THE ANCIENT PALACE

When the foe came at night, unguarded was palace door;

In midcourt golden lotus blooms left trace no more.

At midnight the new emperor did not stop singing;

The ancient palace bells in the breeze still kept ringing.

THE HAN PALACE

The blue bird did not bring elixir from the sky;

In vain the monarch waited in his tower high.

His talented poet thristy for drink divine

Was never given a drop of immortal wine.

BREAKING WILLOW TWIGS AT PARTING

I

What can I do but pour wine for your broken heart?
Don't aggravate your grievous eyebrows and waist slender!
Before our death there's nothing sadder than to part.
Why should the vernal breeze save willow branches tender?

II

Willow leaves drink smoke and mist, unwilling to leave,
And thousands of branches caress the setting sun.
Don't break off all the twigs, O lover, lest it should grieve
Your friend on his return with all trees stripped and done.

PALACE DANCERS

The crystal screens caressed the royal steps of jade;
The dancers vied to show slender waist in brocade.
Although the fish and dragon play might please the Sire,
The musician risked to be killed at his ire.

A PALACE POEM

Imperial favor flows like eastward running stream:

When won, it brings fear for loss; when lost, it brings woe.

Don't sing before winecups the "Fallen Blossom's Dream"

For from Western Palace the cold wind will soon blow.

LOVESICKNESS

At dusk she will not gaze afar in tower high;

The hook-like moon shines on untrodden stairs nearby.

Banana leaves uprolled and lilacs in a knot

Reveal their lovesickness the vernal breeze knows not.

THE SOUTHERN KING'S TRYST WITH THE MOUNTAIN GODDESS

Uphill the palace stands, above the halls a bower,

The stream before the halls carries twilight away.

The evening sky brings fresh shower for thirsting flower.

How could the griefless poet without sorrow stay?

PARTING AT MORNING ON THE WOODEN BRIDGE

The Milky Way fades over the high city wall;

The parting pavilion overlooks the rippling stream.

The fairy riding a carp goes up the waterfall,

Leaving the lotus bloom shed red tears in her dream.

PLAYING ON FLUTE IN SIGHT OF THE SILVER RIVER

Gazing on Milky Way, on flute of jade I play

In bower and courtyard cold near the break of day.

Gone are sweet dreams in heavy quilt of bygone year;

A lonely bird on lonely tree shivers with fear.

Fragrance of moonlit bower spreads out with the rain;

Flickering candle flame and frost sing the refrain.

Why should you go on crane divine to Heaven high?

The music played by queens would bring you to the sky.

SPRING RAIN

Gloomy in early spring, I lie still clad in white;

How much I miss our rendezvous now in sad plight!

Your rosy bower chills my heart when viewed in rain;

Back when dim lamplight is screened, lonely I remain.

Far on your way, you should be grieved when spring is late;

Deep in the night, I but dimly dream of my mate.

How could I send my love-letter with two jade rings?

Could miles of clouds be pierced by a swan on the wings?

A SUNNY EVENING AFTER RAIN

I look down on town wall from my retreat;

With spring just gone, summer weather is clear.

It's Heaven's will to pity green grass sweet;

In human world sunny evening's held dear.

I can see afar from my tower high;

The parting rays make my small window bright.

The Southern birds find their nest again dry;

When they fly back, they feel their bodies light.

ON THE TOWER OF THE CITY WALL

From hundred-foot-high city wall I look afar;

Beyond green willow branches sandy islets are.

I remember a scholar while young shed vain tears,

And a famed scholar roamed in the spring of his years.

I can't forget white-haired General on the lake floating,

After changing the face of the world he went boating.

An owl might feed on dead rats with good appetite,

But a phoenix would perch on trees of lofty height.

THE END OF THE SKY

Spring is far, far away

Where the sun slants its ray.

If orioles have tear,

Wet highest flowers here!

FROM DAY TO DAY

From day to day in splendor spring with sunlight vies,

The sloping hillside way sweet with apricot bloom.

When could my heart-string be as free from worldly ties

As the hundred-foot-long gossamer in the gloom?

DRAGON POOL FEAST

At Dragon Pool feast spread screens embroidered with cloud,

All music drowned in the emperor's drumbeats loud.

Come back at midnight to hear the waterclock's song,

The solitary prince lay awake all night long.

(Note) Lady Yang, former wife of the prince, became the Emperor's
favorite mistress.

TO THE ROVING ORIOLE

Oriole roving high and low,

Are you happy o'er fields and streams?

What does your warbling want to show?

Can the fine days fulfil your dreams?

You are careless of shine or rain,

Dawn or dusk, open or closed door.

I'm grieved to hear your sad refrain,

When spring is gone and blooms no more.

TO THE MOON GODDESS

Upon the marble screen the candlelight is winking;
The Silver River slants and morning stars are sinking.
You'd regret to have stolen the miraculous potion:
Each night you brood o'er the lonely celestial ocean.

TWO UNTITLED POEMS

I

On manifold silk canopy with phoenix tail
She stitches green patterns in the deep of night.
Shy looked her face the moon-shaped fan could hardly veil;
Gone was his rolling cab, speechless, soon lost to sight.
The lonely candle sheds its dim light to deplore;
Red pomegranates see her wait for news with zest.
His dappled horse is tethered to the willow shore.
When can she enjoy the good wind from the southwest?

II

The grievous curtains hang deep in her Griefless Hall;

Awake from sleep, she finds the sleepless night grow long.

A happy life in love is a dream beyond call;

A lonely virgin's deprived of amorous song.

Against the wind and waves can't stand her cresses frail.

Will the moon shed dew to make her laurel leaves sweet?

Although she knows her lovesickness of no avail,

How can a passionate poor heart no longer beat?

A BRIGHT SCHOLAR

The emperor recalled the banished scholar bright,

Peerless in eloquence and in ability.

Alas! His Majesty drew near him at midnight

To consult not on man but on divinity.

CHEN TAO

THE RIVERSIDE BATTLEGROUND

They would lay down their lives to wipe away the Huns;

They've bit the dust, five thousand sable-clad brave sons.

Alas! Their bones lie on riverside battleground,

But in dreams of their wives they still seem safe and sound.

LI QUNYU

TO A DESERTED LOVER

Your literary fame was once loved best;

Your muse then came in dreams to lovebirds' nest.

We cannot rule o'er fickle cloud or shower.

So let it water any thirsting flower!

Cao Ye

THE RATS IN THE PUBLIC GRANARY

The rats in the public granary so fatted grow;

When they see man come in, they do not run away.

The soldiers not provided, and people hungry go.

Who allows the rats to eat so much from day to day?

Zhao Gu

ON THE RIVERSIDE TOWER

Alone I mount the Riverside Tower and sigh

To see the moonbeams blend with waves and waves with the sky.

Last year I came to view the moon with my compeers.

But where are they now that the scene is like last year's?

CUI JUE

ELEGY ON LI SHANGYIN

In vain you could have soared to the azure sky;

Before your long, long wings are fully spread, you die.

The birds bewail with fallen flowers: "Where are you?"

The phoenix won't alight when dead is the bamboo.

A steed may be crippled if ridden by a cur;

The lutist broke his lute without a connoisseur.

In nether world not sun or moon or stars in sight,

You are the brightest star in the eternal night.

LUO YIN

TO A FAIR DANCER

Drunken, we parted here more than ten years ago;

Again I meet you as light a dancer as then.

You are not married and my fame remains still low;

Maybe we are not equal to all other men.

FOR MYSELF

Sing when you're happy, and from worries keep away!
How can we bear so much regret and so much sorrow?
When you have wine to drink, O drink your fill today!
Should sorrow come, alas! tell it to come tomorrow!

TO THE PARROT

Do not complain of golden cage and wings cut short;
The southern land is far warmer than the northwest.
Don't clearly speak if you listen to my exhort!
You will offend if clearly your complaint's expressed.

SNOW

All say that snow forebodes a bumper year.
What if it should arouse less joy than fear?
There are poor people in the capital,
Who are afraid much bumper snow will fall.

WEI ZHUANG

BYGONE DAYS

I'd visited the capital in bygone days:
The bowers filled with midnight songs and clear moon rays.
Candlelight shed on trees lengthened evening hours;
No autumn ever came among dewy peach flowers.
The noble son of west garden had a free hand;
The beauty knew no sorrow in the southern land.
Now the state torn by war, all's turned into a dream;
The setting sun sees only the east-flowing stream.

THE LAKESIDE LAND

Over the riverside grass falls a drizzling rain;

Six Dynasties have passed like dreams, birds cry in vain.

Three miles along the dike unfeeling willows stand,

Adorning like a veil of mist the lakeside land.

NIE YIZHONG

POOR PEASANTS

Up in old fields the fathers toil;

Down in new fields the sons break soil.

The corn in sixth moon still in blade,

Government granaries are made.

Zhang Jie

The Pit Where Emperor Qin Burned the Classics

Smoke of burnt classics gone up with the empire's fall,
Fortresses and rivers could not guard the capital.
Before the pit turned cold, eastern rebellions spread;
The leaders of revolts were not scholars well read.

Cao Song

A Year of War

The lakeside country has become a battleground.
How can the peasants and woodmen live all around?
I pray you not to talk about the glories vain;
A victor's fame is built on thousands of men slain.

Han Wo

A Lonely Woman

On the mid-court the moon sheds a pale light
And petals float down from crabapple trees.
On vacant steps she fixes her lonely sight
Only to see the swing sway in the breeze.

Du Xunhe

A Widow Living in the Mountains

Her husband killed in war, she lives in a thatched hut,
Wearing coarse hempen clothes and a flaxen hair.
She should pay taxes though down mulberries were cut,
And before harvest though fields and gardens lie bare.
She has to eat wild herbs together with their root,
And burn as fuel leafy branches from the trees.
However deep she hides in mountains as a brute,
From oppressive taxes she can never be free.

HUANG CHAO

TO THE CHRYSANTHEMUM

In soughing western wind you blossom far and nigh;
Your fragrance is too cold to invite butterfly.
Some day if I as Lord of Spring come into power,
I'd order you to bloom together with peach flower.

THE CHRYSANTHEMUM

When autumn comes, the mountain-climbing day is nigh;
My flower blows when other blooms come to an end.
In battle array my fragrance rises sky-high;
The capital with my golden armour will blend.

Wang Jia

A Spring Feast

The paddy crops wax rich at the foot of Goose-lake Hill;
Door half closed, pigs in sty and fowls in cage are still.
The shade of mulberries lengthens, the feast is o'er,
All drunken villagers are helped back to their door.

After the Rain

Before the rain I still see blooming flowers;
Only green leaves are left after the showers.
Over the wall pass butterflies and bees;
I wonder if spring's in my neighbor's trees.

CUI DAORONG

A CLOAK OF SPRING

I try to cut for him a cloak of spring;

My scissors breathe the cold still lingering.

Far colder is the far-off garrison town.

How can he not expect a warrior's gown!

QIN TAOYU

A POOR MAID

In thatched hut I know not fragrant silks and brocade;

To be married I can't find a good go-between.

Who would love an uncommon fashion though self-made?

All pity my simple toilet and humble mien.

I dare boast my fingers' needlework without peer,

But I won't vie with maidens painting eyebrows long.

I regret to stitch golden thread from year to year,

But to make wedding gowns which to others belong.

Yu Wuling

TO A PINE-SELLER

Men come to market to seek gain.

Why are you so sincere in vain?

You sell creekside tree without flower

To those who live in emerald bower.

Its leaves are meager under snow,

Its pale blooms e'en in spring won't blow.

The rich love but peach and plum sweet;

Dusted pines can't be sold in the street.

Pi Rixiu

LAMENT OF AN ACORN-EATER

Acorns ripen in autumn cold;

Falling into scrubs, they seem lost.

A hunched gray-haired woman old

Gathers them, treading morning frost.

To get a handful will take long;

To fill her basket needs a day.

She suns and steams them — Is she strong? —

In winter her hunger to stay.

By hillside there's ripening rice,

From purple spikes fragrance pervades.

She reaps and hulls the grain so nice,

Each kernel like an earring of jade.

She takes the grain the tax to pay;

Not much is left for her to store.

How can the tax-collecter say

She has paid but half and no more!

Officials would commit a crime;

Taking bribes, greedy ones are worse.

Peasants owe them debt in busy time,

But debt paid goes to private purse.

From winter even into spring

She has only acorns to eat.

I've heard the premier helped the king

To give more and take less to cheat.

Seeing this woman old, can I

Keep back tears streaming from the eye?

ZHANG BI

TO MY LOVE

When you were gone, in dreams I lingered you know where:

Our courtyard seemed the same with zigzag balustrade.

Only the sympathetic moon was shining there

O'er fallen petals melting like you into the shade.

ANONYMOUS

THE GOLDEN DRESS

Love not your golden dress, I pray,

More than your youthful golden hours!

Gather sweet blossoms while you may

And not the twig devoid of flowers!

许译中国经典诗文集

唐诗三百首

许渊冲 译

五洲传播出版社 中华书局

序

    21世纪是全球化的世纪。新世纪的新人不但应该了解全球的文化，而且应该使本国文化走向世界，成为全球文化的一部分，使世界文化更加灿烂辉煌。如果说20世纪是美国世纪的话，那么，19世纪可以说是英国世纪，18世纪则是法国世纪。再推上去，自7世纪至13世纪，则可以说是中国世纪或唐宋世纪，因为中国在唐宋六百年间，政治制度先进，经济繁荣，文化发达，是全世界其他国家难以企及的。

    唐代的全盛时期可以说是"礼乐"治国的盛世。根据冯友兰先生的解释，"礼"模仿自然外在的秩序，"乐"模仿自然内在的和谐；"礼"可以养性，"乐"可以怡情；"礼"是"义"的外化，"乐"是"仁"的外化；做人要重"仁义"，治国要重"礼乐"。这是中国屹立于文明世界几千年不衰的重要原因。就以唐玄宗而论，他去泰山时祭奠了孔子，写下了《经鲁祭孔子而叹之》的五言律诗，可见他对礼教的尊重，对士人的推崇。

    因此，唐代文化昌盛，诗人辈出，唐诗成了中国文化的瑰宝。不但是在中国，就是在全世界，正如诺贝尔文学奖评奖委员会主席埃斯普马克说的："世界上哪些作品能与中国的唐诗和《红楼梦》相比的呢？"（《诺贝尔文学奖内幕》306页）

    早在19世纪末期，英国汉学家翟理斯（Giles）曾把唐诗译成韵文，得到评论家的好评，如英国作家斯特莱彻（Strachey）说：翟译唐诗是那个时代最好的诗，在世界文学史上占有独一无二的地位。但20世纪初期英国汉学家韦利

（Waley）认为译诗用韵不可能不因声损义，因此他把唐诗译成自由诗或散体，这就开始了唐诗翻译史上的诗体与散体之争。一般说来，散体译文重真，诗体译文重美，所以散体与诗体之争也可以升华为真与美的矛盾。

唐诗英译真与美之争一直延续到了今天。例如李白的《送友人》就有两种不同的译法，现将原诗和两种译文抄录于下：

> 青山横北郭，白水绕东城。
> 此地一为别，孤蓬万里征。
> 浮云游子意，落日故人情。
> 挥手自兹去，萧萧班马鸣。

(1) Green hills range north of the walled city,

The White River curves along its east.

Once we part here you'll travel far alone,

Like the tumbleweed swept by the autumn wind.

A floating cloud — a wayfarer's feeling from home,

The setting sun — the affection of an old friend.

Waving adieu, as you now depart from me,

Our horses neigh, loath to part from each other.

（《外语教学与研究》1991年第3期）

(2) Blue mountains bar the northern sky;

White water girds the eastern town.

Here is the place to say goodbye;

You'll drift like lonely thistledown.

With floating cloud you'll float away;

Like parting clay I'll part from you.

You wave your hand and go your way;

Your steed still neighs, "Adieu, adieu!"

（香港《中诗英诗比录》133页）

比较一下两种译文，可以说第一种更重真，第二种更重美；第一种更形似，第二种更神似。自然，真和美是相对而言的，往往可以仁者见仁，智者见智。如以第一句而论，"青山"二字，第一种说是绿色的小山，第二种说是蓝色的大山；"北郭"二字，第一种说是城郭的北面，第二种为了避免重复"城"字，把"小城"移到第二行去了，说是北边的天空；由此可见，第一种写的是近景，第二种写的是远景。到底哪种译文更真呢？如以"青山"而论，第二种更形似，如以"北郭"而论，却是第一种更形似。全句最重要的是动词"横"字，第一种译文用了range，是"排列"的意思，读起来像是地理教科书中的术语，重的是真；第二种译文用了bar，作为名词，是"横木"的意思，作为动词，却是像横木一样横在天边，这个词形象生动，气势雄伟，合乎李白的诗风；加上英国诗人济慈在《秋颂》中用过这个词形容云彩，用在这里，更使全句显得诗意盎然，甚至有画龙点睛之妙，可见第二种译文重的是美。

再看第二句，原诗两句对称，"青山"对"白水"，"北郭"对"东城"，具有平衡的形美。第一种译文要求真，"青山"的译文只有两个音节，"白水"却有四个，这就不如第二种译文对称；"北郭"和"东城"的第一种译文也不平衡，没有传达原诗的形美。更重要的还是动词"绕"字，第一种译成curve，作为名词，是曲线的意思，作为动词，则是呈曲线形，这又是一个几何教科书中的术语，读起来仿佛在测量地形，未免大煞风景。第二种译文求美，用了gird一词，使人如见一衣带水的形象，又比第一种译文更有诗情画意了。

原诗第一、二句写景是"起"，第三句"此地"二

211

字是"承"，"为别"二字"转"入叙事，只是时空状语从句，第四句才是主句，转为写情。第一种译文把三、四句合译，把"万里"浅化为far（远），"孤"字等化为alone（孤独）移到第三句去；第四句只把"蓬"字等化为tumbleweed，却把"征"字深化为swept by the autumn wind（秋风横扫），这是求真呢？还是求美呢？可以商榷。据第一位译者研究，这首诗是李白送崔宗之写的。"崔家在嵩山之南，邀李同往，李因急于回家未从。李送走崔……"这样看来，友人并不是被迫离乡背井的，用秋风扫落叶的形象来描写，是译者自己的创造，恐怕不能算真了。能不能说比第二种译文更美呢？第二种译文的第四句借景抒情，把友人比作要"万里征"的"孤蓬"，惜别之心已经形象化了，可以说意美胜过第一种译文。至于音美，第一种译文没有押韵，各行音节数月不等，有长有短；第二种译文却隔行押韵，每行八个音节，都是抑扬格音步，没有"因声损义"，而第一种反倒不押韵而损义了！

第五、六句是全诗的高潮，是抒写离情别恨的妙句。李白善于借景写情，如"请君试问东流水，别意与之谁短长？""桃花潭水深千尺，不及汪伦送我情"，都是借流水、深潭来抒写离别的深情厚意的。在《送友人》中又把惜别之心形象化为浮云和落日，更加显得依依不舍。第一种译文把"意"字译成feeling，把"情"字译成affection，译文形似，似乎忠实于原文。但"情""意"在中文是单音节，在诗词中常用，所以具有一种情韵美或意美。译成英文的对等词，因为在英诗中不如在中国诗词中常用，不能引起情韵的美感。例如"别意与之谁短长？""不及汪伦送我情"等句的英译文是：

(1) O ask the river flowing to the east, I pray,

   Whether its parting grief or mine will longer stay!

(2) However deep the Lake of Peach Blossoms may be,

   It's not so deep, O Wang Lun! as your love for me.

如把grief（"意"）换成feeling，把love（"情"）换成affection，那散文味就太重，诗意却消失了。

第二种译文没有译"情""意"二字，却重复了float和part两个词，说成你和浮云一同飘然而去，我像落日一样离开了你。译文虽不形似，却说出了诗人的离情别意，可以说是一种创造性的翻译，"落日"也换成"正在消逝的白日"了。有人也许会说："孤蓬万里征"中的"征"解释为"秋风横扫"不也是创造性的翻译吗？朱光潜《诗论》104页上说"'从心所欲，不逾矩'是一切艺术的成熟境界"，我看也是翻译艺术的成熟境界。创造性的翻译"从心所欲"，但是不能超越作者的原意。"浮云"和"落日"的第二种译文只是超越了原文的形式，却没有违反原诗的内容，并没有"逾矩"；"秋风横扫"却超越了原文的内容和形式，"逾矩"了，所以我看不能算创造性的翻译。

最后一句"萧萧班马鸣"，第一种译文说是两匹马，第二种说是一匹，到底是几匹马呢？我看这不是"真"，而是"美"的问题。试问到底是两马齐鸣，难舍难分，还是人已萧然而去，只闻萧萧马鸣，更加意味深远悠长，仿佛余音在耳，久久不绝呢？我觉得两马更像"教坊犹奏别离歌"，不如一马"黯然销魂者，唯别而已矣"。还有"萧萧"二字，第一种译文说是难舍难分，马犹如此，人何以堪！第二种却重复了adieu（再见），这是不是"从心所欲"，将马拟人，"逾矩"了呢？我觉得译诗要使读者

"知之，好之，乐之"。如果读者理解了原诗的内容，喜欢译诗的表达方式，读来感到乐趣，那么，"从心所欲"的翻译就不算"逾矩"，甚至可能成为"青出于蓝而胜于蓝"的译文。这样一来，译文就可以说是在和原文竞赛，看哪种形式更能表达原文的内容了。

真与美的矛盾可以说是科学与艺术的矛盾。自然，科学和艺术也有统一的时候，那翻译的问题不大。我和科学家杨振宁1938年在西南联大同学；60年后，我们在清华大学会面，他问我有没有翻译晏几道的《鹧鸪天》"从别后，忆相逢"？我就给他看"歌尽桃花扇影风"的英译文，他说不对，他记得是"扇底风"。在我看来，"扇底风"是实写，"扇影风"是想像，这就是真与美的矛盾，可以看出科学和艺术的不同。

《杨振宁文选》英文本序言中引用了两句杜甫的名诗"文章千古事，得失寸心知"；振宁的英译文是：

1. A piece of literature is meant for the millennium.

   But its ups and downs are known already in the
   author's heart.

译文精确，是典型的科学家风格，但是音节太多，不宜入诗；如果要按艺术风格来译，可以翻译如下：

2. A poem may long, long remain.

   Who knows the poet's loss and gain!

3. A poem lasts a thousand years.

   Who knows the poet's smiles and tears!

比较一下三种译文，"文章"二字，第一种译得最正确；但杜甫并没有写过多少文章，他说的是"文"，指的是"诗"，所以第二、三种就译成poem了。"千古"二字，也是第一种最精确，第三种说"千年"，也算正确，第二种只说long（长久），就太泛了。"千古事"是流传千古的事，以意美而论，是第一种译得好；以音美和形美而论，却是第二、三种更合音律。"得失"二字，第二种译得最形似，但是并不明确；第一种译成ups and downs，更注意文章的客观作用，第三种译成笑和泪，更强调主观的感受。"寸心知"三字，第一种理解为作者有自知之明，第二、三种却理解为有谁知诗人之心了。

从李白、杜甫诗的译例看来，可以说科学派的译文更重"三似"：形似、意似、神似；艺术派的译文更重"三美"：意美、音美、形美。科学派常用对等的译法；艺术派则常用"三化"的译法：等化、浅化、深化。科学派的目的是使读者知之；艺术派则认为"知之"是低标准，高标准应该是"三之"：知之、好之、乐之。一般说来，诗是具有意美、音美、形美的文字，就是英国诗人柯尔律治（Coleridge）说的the best words in the best order（见《英诗格律及自由诗》扉页，下同）。美国诗人弗洛斯特（Frost）却认为诗是"说一指二"的（saying one thing and meaning another）。这就是说，原诗是最好的文字，译成对等的文字，却不一定是最好的诗句，这时就要舍"对等"而求"最好"，也就是要发挥译语的优势，即充分利用译语最好的表达方式，而不是对等的表达方式。如"得失"的对等词是gain and loss，但ups and downs或smiles and tears却是更好的表达方式。换句话说，在原文说一指一的时候，对等的译文不但形似，而且意似，甚至可以神似；如果原文说一指二，那形似或等化的译文就不可能神似，应该试用浅化或深化的译法，才有可能传达原诗的意美、音美、形美。总而言之一句话，就是要用再创的译法，例如把"得失"说成"啼笑"。这种"再创"不是内容等于形式，或

215

一加一等于二的科学方法，而是内容大于形式，一加一大于二的艺术方法。所以我认为文学翻译，尤其是译诗，不是一种科学，而是一种艺术。从某种意义上来讲，文学翻译甚至可以看成是译语之间或译语和原语之间的竞赛，看哪种语文更能表达原语的内容。其实，这种竞赛在人类文化史上是不断进行的。如三千年前的特洛亚战争，经过多少行吟诗人竞相歌唱，最后荷马取得胜利。两百年前，查普曼、蒲伯等诗人把荷马史诗译成英文，这是新的竞赛，又取得了新的胜利。从更广泛的意义来说，有一些莎士比亚的作品也是英语和原语的竞赛，例如《哈姆雷特》原是丹麦的故事，《罗密欧与朱丽叶》是威尼斯的故事，但是莎士比亚的英语赛过了原语的传说。到了17世纪，德莱顿把莎士比亚的《安东尼与克丽奥佩特拉》改写成《一切为了爱情》，这又是在和莎士比亚竞赛，当时的贵族观众认为胜过莎剧，后世的平民观众却认为不如莎剧宏伟。不管谁胜谁负，或者难分高下，这不都是竞赛吗？而人类的文化就在不断的竞赛中不断前进了。

《唐诗三百首》是中国文化的精粹。早在1929年，美国就出版了宾纳（Bynner）的译本，基本上用的是艺术译法。到1973年，台北又出版了英国译者赫尔登（Herdan）的译本，基本上用的是科学译法。但是两种译本都没有用韵，不能传达唐诗的意美、音美、形美。到1987年，香港才出版我和陆佩弦、吴钧陶等合译的《唐诗三百首新译》，基本上是韵文，得到国内外的好评和批评。如《记钱钟书先生》341页上说：《唐诗》及论译"二书如羽翼之相辅，星月之交辉，足征非知者不能行，非行者不能知"。菲律宾《联合日报》1994年2月3日评论说：《唐诗三百首》中许译"一百多首，炉火纯青；其他译者，多数译法与他相似，程度参差"。因此，我觉得香港本《唐诗三百首》有修订甚至重译的必要。

1994年英国企鹅图书公司出版了我英译的《中国不朽诗三百首》，美国宾州大学顾毓琇教授读后说："历代诗、词、曲译成英文，且能押韵自然，功力过人，实为有史以来第一。"（见1997年5月23日《信息报》）同年，湖南出版社《楚辞》英译本得到墨尔本大学美国学者好评，说是"当算英美文学里的一座高峰"（见1998年版Vanished Springs封底）。1992年外文出版社出了《西厢记》英译本，英国智慧女神出版社说："在艺术性和吸引力方面，可以和莎士比亚的《罗密欧与朱丽叶》媲美。"（见《中国图书商报》1999年8月31日《书评月刊》）

中国人英译的中国古典文学，怎么能成为英美文学的高峰，甚至可以和莎士比亚媲美呢？钱钟书先生说得好："非知者不能行，非行者不能知。"在我看来，"知"就是理论，"行"就是实践。因为我有了几十年的实践经验，把中国古典文学十大名著译成了英、法两种韵文，因此，我把中国学派的文学翻译理论总结成了十个字："美化之艺术，创优似竞赛。"

所谓"美"，指的是意美、音美、形美。"三美"，这是根据鲁迅在《自文字至文章》一文中所说的："意美以感心，一也；音美以感耳，二也；形美以感目，三也。"不过鲁迅说的是写文章，我把他的理论应用到文学翻译上来了。所谓"化"，是根据钱钟书提出的："文学翻译的最高理想是'化'。"不过我把"化"字扩大为等化、浅化、深化"三化"了。所谓"之"，是根据孔子在《论语》中说的："知之者不如好之者，好之者不如乐之者。"我把知之、好之、乐之应用于文学翻译，就提出了

"三之"论。至于"艺术"二字，那是根据朱光潜提出的："'从心所欲，不逾矩'是一切艺术的成熟境界。"简单说来，"三美"是文学翻译的本体论，"三化"是方法论，"三之"是目的论，"艺术"是认识论，总起来说，就是"美化之艺术"。

我又从郭沫若提出的"好的翻译等于创作"中取了一个"创"字，从傅雷提出的"重神似不重形似"中再取一个"似"字，从我自己提出的"发挥译语优势"中取出一个"优"字，加上"竞赛"二字，就成了"创优似竞赛"。"优"是"三美"合而为一的本体论，"创"是"三化"合而为一的方法论，"似"是"三之"合而为一的目的论，"竞赛"是包含在"艺术"中的认识论。这就是中国学派的文学翻译理论。

世界上有十多亿人用中文，又有约十亿人用英文，所以中文和英文是世界上最重要的文字，中英互译是世界上最重要的翻译。中国有不少能互译的文学翻译家。"非行者不能知"，中国学派的文学翻译理论是今天世界上水平最高的理论，可以把文学翻译提高到创作的地位。这就是说，译著应该等于原作者用译语的创作，一流译者翻出来的文句诗行，读起来和一流作家写出来的作品，应该没有什么差别。

中国学派的翻译原则在20世纪初是严复提出的"信、达、雅"；到了20世纪末，大致可以分为"信、达、切"和"信、达、优"两派，基本上是直译派和意译派，或形似派和神似派。在我看来，"信、达、切"是文学翻译的低标准，如李白《送友人》的第一种英译；"信、达、优"是高标准，如第二种译文。但形似派有人不同意，认为"再创"的译文有损原作者的风格。什么是风格？这是一个仁者见仁、智者见智的问题。《文学翻译原理》96页上说，李白的风格是"飘逸"。但从《送友人》的两种译文看来，哪一种传达了"飘逸"的风格呢？从内容上来看，可以说两种译文都不能算是不"飘逸"的；从形式上来看，可以说第一种译文的字句更切合原文，而第二种译文则传达了原诗的意美、音美、形美，难道能说"三美"不符合原诗的风格么？所以研究文学翻译理论，不能从抽象的"风格"概念出发，而要分析具体的实例，只要译文能使读者知之、好之、乐之，就不必多考虑作者的风格。罗曼•罗兰在《约翰•克里斯托夫》法文本1565页上说："作者有什么重要？只有作品才是真实的。"英国诗人艾略特(Eliot)更说过："个人的才智有限，文化的力量无穷。"（转引自《追忆逝水年华》43页）在我看来，这就是说，民族文化比个人风格重要得多，如果能对人类文化作出贡献，作者的风格应该是次要的。

法籍作家程纪贤在他的获奖作品《天一说》(Le dit de Tianyi) 267页上说："艺术并不模仿自然，结果反倒迫使自然模仿艺术。"这话说得耐人寻味。思索一下，人类从四足有毛的爬行动物进化到两足无毛的直立动物，不就是自然模仿艺术（手艺）的过程吗？同样的道理，翻译开始模仿创作，最后创作反而模仿翻译，"五四"以来新文学的发展不就提供了范例吗？所以文学翻译应该发展为创作的范例，这就是和原作竞赛，甚至超越原作，提高人类的文化。

这本汉英对照《唐诗三百首》就是我用"再创"法重译的选集，所选的篇目和流行的《唐诗三百首》有所不同，主要是我喜欢的并能译成韵文的作品。希望这个新译本和我英译的《楚辞》《西厢记》一样，能使国外读者

219

"知之，好之，乐之"，能使中国文学走向世界，走向21世纪，使新世纪的文化更加光辉灿烂。

荣获诺贝尔奖的几十位科学家1988年在巴黎发表宣言说："人类要继续生存下去，就必须回过头来学习孔子的智慧。"在我看来，孔子的智慧主要表现在"礼乐之治"或"己所不欲，勿施于人"的"礼治"上，这从热爱和平、热爱人生、热爱自然的唐诗中也可以看出。孔子是"圣之时者也"，结合时代，"回过头来学习孔子的智慧"，我认为应该把"礼治"发展为"天下为公，人尽其才"的"理治"。其实，我国提出的和平共处五项原则，就是"己所不欲，勿施于人"发展到今天的国际政治原则。而"知之、好之、乐之"三之论和"从心所欲，不逾矩"的艺术，正是孔子的"礼乐"应用于文学翻译的理论。希望孔子的智慧、唐诗的智慧，能丰富21世纪的全球文化，使全世界都能享受和平、繁荣、幸福的生活。

许渊冲
1999年9月于北京大学

蝉

垂緌饮清露，流响出疏桐。
居高声自远，非是藉秋风。

咏萤

的烁流光小，飘摇弱翅轻。
恐畏无人识，独自暗中明。

落叶

早秋惊落叶，飘零似客心。
翻飞未肯下，犹言惜故林。

过酒家

此日长昏饮，非关养性灵。
眼看人皆醉，何忍独为醒？

野望

东皋薄暮望，徙倚欲何依？
树树皆秋色，山山唯落晖。
牧人驱犊返，猎马带禽归。
相顾无相识，长歌怀采薇。

寒山

杳杳寒山道

杳杳寒山道，落落冷涧滨。
啾啾常有鸟，寂寂更无人。
淅淅风吹面，纷纷雪积身。
朝朝不见日，岁岁不知春。

上官仪

早春桂林殿应诏

步辇出披香，清歌临太液。
晓树流莺满，春堤荒草积。
风光翻露文，雪华上空碧。
花蝶来未已，山光暖将夕。

王勃

送杜少府之任蜀州

城阙辅三秦，风烟望五津。
与君离别意，同是宦游人。
海内存知己，天涯若比邻。
无为在歧路，儿女共沾巾。

滕王阁诗

滕王高阁临江渚，佩玉鸣鸾罢歌舞。
画栋朝飞南浦云，珠帘暮卷西山雨。
闲云潭影日悠悠，物换星移几度秋！
阁中帝子今何在？槛外长江空自流。

杨炯

从军行

烽火照西京，心中自不平。
牙璋辞凤阙，铁骑绕龙城。
雪暗凋旗画，风多杂鼓声。
宁为百夫长，胜作一书生。

骆宾王

在狱咏蝉

西陆蝉声唱，南冠客思深。
不堪玄鬓影，来对白头吟。
露重飞难进，风多响易沉。
无人信高洁，谁为表予心？

韦承庆

南行别弟

澹澹长江水，悠悠远客情。
落花相与恨，到地一无声。

宋之问

渡汉江

岭外音书断，经冬复历春。
近乡情更怯，不敢问来人。

沈佺期

杂诗

闻道黄龙戍，频年不解兵。
可怜闺里月，长在汉家营。
少妇今春意，良人昨夜情。
谁能将旗鼓，一为取龙城？

咏柳

碧玉妆成一树高，万条垂下绿丝绦。
不知细叶谁裁出？二月春风似剪刀。

回乡偶书二首

少小离家老大回，乡音无改鬓毛衰。
儿童相见不相识，笑问客从何处来。

离别家乡岁月多，近来人事半销磨。
惟有门前镜湖水，春风不改旧时波。

登幽州台歌

前不见古人，后不见来者，
念天地之悠悠，独怆然而涕下。

送东莱王学士无竞

宝剑千金买，平生未许人。
怀君万里别，持赠结交亲。
孤松宜晚岁，众木爱芳春。
已矣将何道？无令白发新！

张说

蜀道后期

客心争日月，来往预期程。
秋风不相待，先到洛阳城。

张九龄

望月怀远

海上生明月，天涯共此时。
情人怨遥夜，竟夕起相思。
灭烛怜光满，披衣觉露滋。
不堪盈手赠，还寝梦佳期。

自君之出矣

自君之出矣，不复理残机。
思君如满月，夜夜减清辉。

张旭

山中留客

山光物态弄春晖，莫为轻阴便拟归。
纵使晴明无雨色，入云深处亦沾衣。

李隆基

经鲁祭孔子而叹之

夫子何为者？栖栖一代中。
地犹鄹氏邑，宅即鲁王宫。
叹凤嗟身否，伤麟怨道穷。
今看两楹奠，当与梦时同。

张若虚

春江花月夜

春江潮水连海平，海上明月共潮生。
滟滟随波千万里，何处春江无月明？
江流宛转绕芳甸，月照花林皆似霰。
空里流霜不觉飞，汀上白沙看不见。
江天一色无纤尘，皎皎空中孤月轮。
江畔何人初见月？江月何年初照人？
人生代代无穷已，江月年年只相似。
不知江月照何人，但见长江送流水。
白云一片去悠悠，青枫浦上不胜愁。
谁家今夜扁舟子？何处相思明月楼？
可怜楼上月徘徊，应照离人妆镜台。
玉户帘中卷不去，捣衣砧上拂还来。
此时相望不相闻，愿逐月华流照君。
鸿雁长飞光不度，鱼龙潜跃水成文。

昨夜闲潭梦落花，可怜春半不还家。
江水流春去欲尽，江潭落月复西斜。
斜月沉沉藏海雾，碣石潇湘无限路。
不知乘月几人归？落月摇情满江树。

王湾

次北固山下

客路青山外，行舟绿水前。
潮平两岸阔，风正一帆悬。
海日生残夜，江春入旧年。
乡书何处达？归雁洛阳边。

王翰

凉州词

葡萄美酒夜光杯，欲饮琵琶马上催。
醉卧沙场君莫笑！古来征战几人回？

登鹳雀楼

白日依山尽，黄河入海流。
欲穷千里目，更上一层楼。

凉州词

黄河远上白云间，一片孤城万仞山。
羌笛何须怨杨柳，春风不度玉门关。

夏日南亭怀辛大

山光忽西落，池月渐东上。
散发乘夕凉，开轩卧闲敞。
荷风送香气，竹露滴清响。
欲取鸣琴弹，恨无知音赏。
感此怀故人，中宵劳梦想。

留别王维

寂寂竟何待？朝朝空自归。
欲寻芳草去，惜与故人违。
当路谁相假？知音世所稀。
只应守寂寞，还掩故园扉。

过故人庄

故人具鸡黍，邀我至田家。
绿树村边合，青山郭外斜。
开轩面场圃，把酒话桑麻。
待到重阳日，还来就菊花。

春晓

春眠不觉晓，处处闻啼鸟。
夜来风雨声，花落知多少！

宿建德江

移舟泊烟渚，日暮客愁新。
野旷天低树，江清月近人。

李颀

古从军行

白日登山望烽火，黄昏饮马傍交河。
行人刁斗风沙暗，公主琵琶幽怨多。
野营万里无城郭，雨雪纷纷连大漠。
胡雁哀鸣夜夜飞，胡儿眼泪双双落。
闻道玉门犹被遮，应将性命逐轻车。
年年战骨埋荒外，空见葡萄入汉家。

王昌龄

从军行七首（选二）

其四

青海长云暗雪山，孤城遥望玉门关。
黄沙百战穿金甲，不破楼兰终不还。

其五

大漠风尘日色昏，红旗半卷出辕门。
前军夜战洮河北，已报生擒吐谷浑。

出塞

秦时明月汉时关，万里长征人未还。
但使龙城飞将在，不教胡马度阴山。

西宫秋怨

芙蓉不及美人妆，水殿风来珠翠香。
却恨含情掩秋扇，空悬明月待君王。

长信秋词

奉帚平明金殿开，且将团扇共徘徊。
玉颜不及寒鸦色，犹带昭阳日影来。

闺怨

闺中少妇不知愁，春日凝妆上翠楼。
忽见陌头杨柳色，悔教夫婿觅封侯。

芙蓉楼送辛渐

寒雨连江夜入吴，平明送客楚山孤。
洛阳亲友如相问，一片冰心在玉壶。

终南望积雪

终南阴岭秀，积雪浮云端。
林表明霁色，城中增暮寒。

送别

下马饮君酒，问君何所之。
君言不得意，归卧南山陲。
但去莫复问，白云无尽时。

渭川田家

斜光照墟落，穷巷牛羊归。
野老念牧童，倚杖候荆扉。
雉雊麦苗秀，蚕眠桑叶稀。
田夫荷锄至，相见语依依。
即此羡闲逸，怅然吟《式微》。

山居秋暝

空山新雨后，天气晚来秋。
明月松间照，清泉石上流。
竹喧归浣女，莲动下渔舟。
随意春芳歇，王孙自可留。

终南山

太乙近天都，连山接海隅。
白云回望合，青霭入看无。
分野中峰变，阴晴众壑殊。
欲投人处宿，隔水问樵夫。

观猎

风劲角弓鸣，将军猎渭城。
草枯鹰眼疾，雪尽马蹄轻。
忽过新丰市，还归细柳营。
回看射雕处，千里暮云平。

汉江临泛

楚塞三湘接，荆门九派通。
江流天地外，山色有无中。
郡邑浮前浦，波澜动远空。
襄阳好风日，留醉与山翁。

使至塞上

单车欲问边，属国过居延。
征蓬出汉塞，归雁入胡天。
大漠孤烟直，长河落日圆。
萧关逢候骑，都护在燕然。

孟城坳

新家孟城口，古木余衰柳。
来者复为谁？空悲昔人有。

鹿柴

空山不见人，但闻人语响。
返景入深林，复照青苔上。

竹里馆

独坐幽篁里，弹琴复长啸。
深林人不知，明月来相照。

鸟鸣涧

人闲桂花落，夜静春山空。
月出惊山鸟，时鸣春涧中。

山中送别

山中相送罢，日暮掩柴扉。
春草明年绿，王孙归不归？

杂诗

君自故乡来，应知故乡事。
来日绮窗前，寒梅著花未？

相思

红豆生南国，春来发几枝？
愿君多采撷，此物最相思。

山中

荆溪白石出，天寒红叶稀。
山路元无雨，空翠湿人衣。

送春辞

日日人空老，年年春更归。
相欢在尊酒，不用惜花飞。

秋夜曲

桂魄初生秋露微，轻罗已薄未更衣。
银筝夜久殷勤弄，心怯空房不忍归。

九月九日忆山东兄弟

独在异乡为异客，每逢佳节倍思亲。
遥知兄弟登高处，遍插茱萸少一人。

渭城曲

渭城朝雨浥轻尘，客舍青青柳色新。
劝君更尽一杯酒，西出阳关无故人。

送沈子福之江东

杨柳渡头行客稀，罟师荡桨向临圻。
惟有相思似春色，江南江北送君归。

刘眘虚

阙题

道由白云尽，春与青溪长。
时有落花至，远随流水香。
闲门向山路，深柳读书堂。
幽映每白日，清辉照衣裳。

李白

峨眉山月歌

峨眉山月半轮秋，影入平羌江水流。
夜发清溪向三峡，思君不见下渝州。

望庐山瀑布

日照香炉生紫烟，遥看瀑布挂前川。
飞流直下三千尺，疑是银河落九天。

望天门山

天门中断楚江开，碧水东流至此回。
两岸青山相对出，孤帆一片日边来。

长干行

妾发初覆额，折花门前剧。
郎骑竹马来，绕床弄青梅。
同居长干里，两小无嫌猜。
十四为君妇，羞颜未尝开。
低头向暗壁，千唤不一回。
十五始展眉，愿同尘与灰。
常存抱柱信，岂上望夫台！
十六君远行，瞿塘滟滪堆。

五月不可触，猿声天上哀。
门前迟行迹，一一生绿苔。
苔深不能扫，落叶秋风早。
八月蝴蝶黄，双飞西园草。
感此伤妾心，坐愁红颜老。
早晚下三巴，预将书报家。
相迎不道远，直至长风沙。

金陵酒肆留别

风吹柳花满店香，吴姬压酒唤客尝。
金陵子弟来相送，欲行不行各尽觞。
请君试问东流水，别意与之谁短长？

夜下征虏亭

船下广陵去，月明征虏亭。
山花如绣颊，江火似流萤。

静夜思

床前明月光，疑是地上霜。
举头望明月，低头思故乡。

黄鹤楼送孟浩然之广陵

故人西辞黄鹤楼，烟花三月下扬州。
孤帆远影碧空尽，惟见长江天际流。

长相思

长相思，在长安。
络纬秋啼金井阑，微霜凄凄簟色寒。
孤灯不明思欲绝，卷帷望月空长叹。
美人如花隔云端。
上有青冥之高天，下有渌水之波澜。
天长地远魂飞苦，梦魂不到关山难。
长相思，摧心肝。

蜀道难

噫吁嚱，危乎高哉！
蜀道之难，难于上青天。
蚕丛及鱼凫，开国何茫然！
尔来四万八千岁，不与秦塞通人烟。
西当太白有鸟道，可以横绝峨眉巅。
地崩山摧壮士死，然后天梯石栈相钩连。
上有六龙回日之高标，下有冲波逆折之回川。
黄鹤之飞尚不得过，猿猱欲度愁攀援。
青泥何盘盘？百步九折萦岩峦。

扪参历井仰胁息，以手抚膺坐长叹。

问君西游何时还，畏途巉岩不可攀。

但见悲鸟号古木，雄飞雌从绕林间。

又闻子规啼夜月，愁空山。

蜀道之难，难于上青天，使人闻此凋朱颜。

连峰去天不盈尺，枯松倒挂倚绝壁。

飞湍瀑流争喧豗，砯崖转石万壑雷。

其险也如此，嗟尔远道之人胡为乎来哉！

剑阁峥嵘而崔嵬，一夫当关，万夫莫开。

所守或匪亲，化为狼与豺。

朝避猛虎，夕避长蛇。

磨牙吮血，杀人如麻。

锦城虽云乐，不如早还家。

蜀道之难，难于上青天，侧身西望长咨嗟。

行路难

金樽清酒斗十千，玉盘珍羞直万钱。
停杯投箸不能食，拔剑四顾心茫然。
欲渡黄河冰塞川，将登太行雪满山。
闲来垂钓碧溪上，忽复乘舟梦日边。
行路难，行路难，多歧路，今安在？
长风破浪会有时，直挂云帆济沧海。

春思

燕草如碧丝，秦桑低绿枝。
当君怀归日，是妾断肠时。
春风不相识，何事入罗帷？

长门怨

桂殿长愁不记春，黄金四屋起秋尘。
夜悬明镜青天上，独照长门宫里人。

子夜吴歌

长安一片月，万户捣衣声。
秋风吹不尽，总是玉关情。
何日平胡虏，良人罢远征？

将进酒

君不见黄河之水天上来，奔流到海不复回！
君不见高堂明镜悲白发，朝如青丝暮成雪！
人生得意须尽欢，莫使金樽空对月。
天生我材必有用，千金散尽还复来。
烹羊宰牛且为乐，会须一饮三百杯。
岑夫子，丹丘生，将进酒，杯莫停。
与君歌一曲，请君为我倾耳听。
钟鼓馔玉不足贵，但愿长醉不复醒。
古来圣贤皆寂寞，惟有饮者留其名。
陈王昔时宴平乐，斗酒十千恣欢谑。
主人何为言少钱？径须沽取对君酌。
五花马，千金裘，
呼儿将出换美酒，与尔同销万古愁。

月下独酌

花间一壶酒，独酌无相亲。
举杯邀明月，对影成三人。
月既不解饮，影徒随我身。
暂伴月将影，行乐须及春。
我歌月徘徊，我舞影零乱。
醒时同交欢，醉后各分散。
永结无情游，相期邈云汉。

戏赠杜甫

饭颗山头逢杜甫，头戴笠子日卓午。
借问别来太瘦生，总为从前作诗苦。

梦游天姥吟留别

海客谈瀛洲，烟涛微茫信难求。
越人语天姥，云霞明灭或可睹。
天姥连天向天横，势拔五岳掩赤城。
天台一万八千丈，对此欲倒东南倾。
我欲因之梦吴越，一夜飞度镜湖月。
湖月照我影，送我至剡溪。
谢公宿处今尚在，渌水荡漾清猿啼。
脚著谢公屐，身登青云梯。
半壁见海日，空中闻天鸡。
千岩万转路不定，迷花倚石忽已暝。
熊咆龙吟殷岩泉，栗深林兮惊层巅。
云青青兮欲雨，水澹澹兮生烟。
列缺霹雳，丘峦崩摧。
洞天石扇，訇然中开。
青冥浩荡不见底，日月照耀金银台。
霓为衣兮风为马，云之君兮纷纷而来下。
虎鼓瑟兮鸾回车，仙之人兮列如麻。

忽魂悸以魄动，恍惊起而长嗟。
惟觉时之枕席，失向来之烟霞。
世间行乐亦如此，古来万事东流水。
别君去兮何时还？
且放白鹿青崖间，须行即骑访名山。
安能摧眉折腰事权贵，使我不得开心颜！

劳劳亭

天下伤心处，劳劳送客亭。
春风知别苦，不遣柳条青。

苏台览古

旧苑荒台杨柳新，菱歌清唱不胜春。
只今惟有西江月，曾照吴王宫里人。

越中览古

越王勾践破吴归，义士还家尽锦衣。
宫女如花满春殿，只今惟有鹧鸪飞。

越女词

镜湖水如月，耶溪女如雪。
新妆荡新波，光景两奇绝。

山中问答

问余何意栖碧山，笑而不答心自闲。
桃花流水窅然去，别有天地非人间。

自遣

对酒不觉暝，落花盈我衣。
醉起步溪月，鸟还人亦稀。

独坐敬亭山

众鸟高飞尽，孤云独去闲。
相看两不厌，只有敬亭山。

宣州谢朓楼饯别校书叔云

弃我去者，昨日之日不可留。
乱我心者，今日之日多烦忧。
长风万里送秋雁，对此可以酣高楼。
蓬莱文章建安骨，中间小谢又清发。
俱怀逸兴壮思飞，欲上青天览明月。
抽刀断水水更流，举杯消愁愁更愁。
人生在世不称意，明朝散发弄扁舟。

送友人

青山横北郭，白水绕东城。
此地一为别，孤蓬万里征。
浮云游子意，落日故人情。
挥手自兹去，萧萧班马鸣。

秋浦歌

白发三千丈，缘愁似个长。
不知明镜里，何处得秋霜？

赠汪伦

李白乘舟将欲行，忽闻岸上踏歌声。
桃花潭水深千尺，不及汪伦送我情。

早发白帝城

朝辞白帝彩云间，千里江陵一日还。
两岸猿声啼不住，轻舟已过万重山。

与夏十二登岳阳楼

楼观岳阳尽，川迥洞庭开。
雁引愁心去，山衔好月来。
云间连下榻，天上接行杯。
醉后凉风起，吹人舞袖回。

宿五松山下荀媪家

我宿五松下，寂寥无所欢。
田家秋作苦，邻女夜春寒。
跪进雕胡饭，月光明素盘。
令人惭漂母，三谢不能餐。

哭宣城善酿纪叟

纪叟黄泉里，还应酿老春。
夜台无李白，沽酒与何人？

临终歌

大鹏飞兮振八裔，中天摧兮力不济。
余风激兮万世，游扶桑兮挂左袂。
后人得之传此，仲尼亡兮谁为出涕？

徐安贞

闻邻家理筝

北斗横天夜欲阑，愁人倚月思无端。
忽闻画阁秦筝逸，知是邻家赵女弹。
曲成虚忆青蛾敛，调急遥怜玉指寒。
银锁重关听未辟，不如眠去梦中看。

崔颢

黄鹤楼

昔人已乘黄鹤去，此地空余黄鹤楼。
黄鹤一去不复返，白云千载空悠悠。
晴川历历汉阳树，芳草萋萋鹦鹉洲。
日暮乡关何处是？烟波江上使人愁。

长干曲

一

君家何处住？妾住在横塘。
停船暂借问，或恐是同乡。

二

家临九江水，来去九江侧。
同是长干人，生小不相识。

金昌绪

春怨

打起黄莺儿，莫教枝上啼！
啼时惊妾梦，不得到辽西。

崔国辅

吴声子夜歌

净扫黄金阶，飞霜皎如雪。
下帘弹箜篌，不忍见秋月。

破山寺后禅院

清晨入古寺，初日照高林。
曲径通幽处，禅房花木深。
山光悦鸟性，潭影空人心。
万籁此俱寂，但余钟磬音。

燕歌行

汉家烟尘在东北，汉将辞家破残贼。
男儿本自重横行，天子非常赐颜色。
扰金伐鼓下榆关，旌旆逶迤碣石间。
校尉羽书飞瀚海，单于猎火照狼山。
山川萧条极边土，胡骑凭陵杂风雨。
战士军前半死生，美人帐下犹歌舞。
大漠穷秋塞草腓，孤城落日斗兵稀。
身当恩遇恒轻敌，力尽关山未解围。
铁衣远戍辛勤久，玉箸应啼别离后。
少妇城南欲断肠，征人蓟北空回首。
边庭飘飖那可度？绝域苍茫更何有！
杀气三时作阵云，寒声一夜传刁斗。
相看白刃血纷纷，死节从来岂顾勋？
君不见沙场征战苦，至今犹忆李将军！

别董大

千里黄云白日曛，北风吹雁雪纷纷。
莫愁前路无知己！天下谁人不识君？

储光羲

钓鱼湾

垂钓绿湾春，春深杏花乱。
潭清疑水浅，荷动知鱼散。
日暮待情人，维舟绿杨岸。

刘长卿

逢雪宿芙蓉山主人

日暮苍山远，天寒白屋贫。
柴门闻犬吠，风雪夜归人。

送灵澈上人

苍苍竹林寺，杳杳钟声晚。
荷笠带夕阳，青山独归远。

早梅

一树寒梅白玉条，迥临村路傍溪桥。
不知近水花先发，疑是经冬雪未销。

五日观妓

西施漫道浣春纱，碧玉今时斗丽华。
眉黛夺将萱草色，红裙妒杀石榴花。
新歌一曲令人艳，醉舞双眸敛鬓斜。
谁道五丝能续命，却令今日死君家！

望岳

岱宗夫如何？齐鲁青未了。
造化钟神秀，阴阳割分晓。
荡胸生层云，决眦入飞鸟。
会当凌绝顶，一览众山小。

兵车行

车辚辚，马萧萧，行人弓箭各在腰。
耶娘妻子走相送，尘埃不见咸阳桥。
牵衣顿足拦道哭，哭声直上干云霄。
道旁过者问行人，行人但云点行频。
或从十五北防河，便至四十西营田。
去时里正与裹头，归来头白还戍边。
边庭流血成海水，武皇开边意未已。
君不闻汉家山东二百州，千村万落生荆杞。
纵有健妇把锄犁，禾生陇亩无东西。
况复秦兵耐苦战，被驱不异犬与鸡。
长者虽有问，役夫敢申恨？
且如今年冬，未休关西卒。
县官急索租，租税从何出？
信知生男恶，反是生女好。
生女犹得嫁比邻，生男埋没随百草。
君不见，青海头，古来白骨无人收。
新鬼烦冤旧鬼哭，天阴雨湿声啾啾。

赠李白

秋来相顾尚飘蓬，未就丹砂愧葛洪。
痛饮狂歌空度日，飞扬跋扈为谁雄？

饮中八仙歌（节选）

李白斗酒诗百篇，长安市上酒家眠。
天子呼来不上船，自称臣是酒中仙。

前出塞

挽弓当挽强，用箭当用长。
射人先射马，擒贼先擒王。
杀人亦有限，列国自有疆。
苟能制侵陵，岂在多杀伤？

自京赴奉先县咏怀（节选）

朱门酒肉臭，路有冻死骨。
荣枯咫尺异，惆怅难再述。

月夜

今夜鄜州月，闺中只独看。
遥怜小儿女，未解忆长安。
香雾云鬟湿，清辉玉臂寒。
何时倚虚幌，双照泪痕干？

春望

国破山河在，城春草木深。
感时花溅泪，恨别鸟惊心。
烽火连三月，家书抵万金。
白头搔更短，浑欲不胜簪。

哀江头

少陵野老吞声哭，春日潜行曲江曲。
江头宫殿锁千门，细柳新蒲为谁绿？
忆昔霓旌下南苑，苑中万物生颜色。
昭阳殿里第一人，同辇随君侍君侧。
辇前才人带弓箭，白马嚼啮黄金勒。
翻身向天仰射云，一笑正坠双飞翼。
明眸皓齿今何在？血污游魂归不得！
清渭东流剑阁深，去住彼此无消息。
人生有情泪沾臆，江水江花岂终极？
黄昏胡骑尘满城，欲往城南望城北。

羌村

峥嵘赤云西，日脚下平地。
柴门鸟雀噪，归客千里至。
妻孥怪我在，惊定还拭泪。
世乱遭飘荡，生还偶然遂。
邻人满墙头，感叹亦歔欷。
夜阑更秉烛，相对如梦寐。

独立

空外一鸷鸟，河间双白鸥。
飘飖搏击便，容易往来游。
草露亦多湿，蛛丝仍未收。
天机近人事，独立万端忧。

赠卫八处士

人生不相见，动如参与商。
今夕复何夕？共此灯烛光。
少壮能几时？鬓发各已苍。
访旧半为鬼，惊呼热中肠。
焉知二十载，重上君子堂？
昔别君未婚，儿女忽成行。

怡然敬父执，问我来何方？
问答乃未已，驱儿罗酒浆。
夜雨剪春韭，新炊间黄粱。
主称会面难，一举累十觞。
十觞亦不醉，感子故意长。
明日隔山岳，世事两茫茫。

石壕吏

暮投石壕村，有吏夜捉人。
老翁逾墙走，老妇出门看。
吏呼一何怒！妇啼一何苦！
听妇前致词："三男邺城戍。
一男附书至，二男新战死。
存者且偷生，死者长已矣！
室中更无人，惟有乳下孙。
有孙母未去，出入无完裙。
老妪力虽衰，请从吏夜归。
急应河阳役，犹得备晨炊。"
夜久语声绝，如闻泣幽咽。
天明登前途，独与老翁别。

梦李白

死别已吞声，生别常恻恻。
江南瘴疬地，逐客无消息。
故人入我梦，明我长相忆。
君今在罗网，何以有羽翼？
恐非平生魂，路远不可测。
魂来枫林青，魂返关塞黑。
落月满屋梁，犹疑照颜色。
水深波浪阔，无使蛟龙得！

月夜忆舍弟

戍鼓断人行，边秋一雁声。
露从今夜白，月是故乡明。
有弟皆分散，无家问死生。
寄书长不达，况乃未休兵！

病马

乘尔亦已久，天寒关塞深。
尘中老尽力，岁晚病伤心。
毛骨岂殊众？驯良犹至今。
物微意不浅，感动一沉吟。

蜀相

丞相祠堂何处寻？锦官城外柏森森。
映阶碧草自春色，隔叶黄鹂空好音。
三顾频烦天下计，两朝开济老臣心。
出师未捷身先死，长使英雄泪满襟。

江村

清江一曲抱村流，长夏江村事事幽。
自去自来堂上燕，相亲相近水中鸥。
老妻画纸为棋局，稚子敲针作钓钩。
但有故人供禄米，微躯此外更何求？

客至

舍南舍北皆春水，但见群鸥日日来。
花径不曾缘客扫，蓬门今始为君开。
盘飧市远无兼味，樽酒家贫只旧醅。
肯与邻翁相对饮，隔篱呼取尽余杯。

漫兴

肠断春江欲尽头，杖藜徐步立芳洲。
颠狂柳絮随风舞，轻薄桃花逐水流。

春夜喜雨

好雨知时节，当春乃发生。
随风潜入夜，润物细无声。
野径云俱黑，江船火独明。
晓看红湿处，花重锦官城。

茅屋为秋风所破歌

八月秋高风怒号，卷我屋上三重茅。
茅飞渡江洒江郊，高者挂罥长林梢，
下者飘转沉塘坳。
南村群童欺我老无力，忍能对面为盗贼，
公然抱茅入竹去。
唇焦口燥呼不得，归来倚杖自叹息。
俄顷风定云墨色，秋天漠漠向昏黑。
布衾多年冷似铁，骄儿恶卧踏里裂。
床头屋漏无干处，雨脚如麻未断绝。
自经丧乱少睡眠，长夜沾湿何由彻！
安得广厦千万间，大庇天下寒士俱欢颜，
风雨不动安如山！
呜呼！
何时眼前突兀见此屋，
吾庐独破受冻死亦足！

赠花卿

锦城丝管日纷纷，半入江风半入云。
此曲只应天上有，人间能得几回闻？

戏为六绝句（选一）

王杨卢骆当时体，轻薄为文哂未休。
尔曹身与名俱灭，不废江河万古流。

闻官军收河南河北

剑外忽传收蓟北，初闻涕泪满衣裳。
却看妻子愁何在，漫卷诗书喜欲狂。
白首放歌须纵酒，青春作伴好还乡。
即从巴峡穿巫峡，便下襄阳向洛阳。

绝句

江碧鸟逾白，山青花欲燃。
今春看又过，何日是归年？

绝句

两个黄鹂鸣翠柳，一行白鹭上青天。
窗含西岭千秋雪，门泊东吴万里船。

旅夜书怀

细草微风岸，危樯独夜舟。
星垂平野阔，月涌大江流。
名岂文章著？官应老病休。
飘飘何所似？天地一沙鸥。

八阵图

功盖三分国，名成八阵图。
江流石不转，遗恨失吞吴。

江上

江上日多雨，萧萧荆楚秋。
高风下木叶，永夜揽貂裘。
勋业频看镜，行藏独倚楼。
时危思报主，衰谢不能休。

秋兴

玉露凋伤枫树林，巫山巫峡气萧森。
江间波浪兼天涌，塞上风云接地阴。
丛菊两开他日泪，孤舟一系故园心。
寒衣处处催刀尺，白帝城高急暮砧。

登高

风急天高猿啸哀，渚清沙白鸟飞回。
无边落木萧萧下，不尽长江滚滚来。
万里悲秋常作客，百年多病独登台。
艰难苦恨繁霜鬓，潦倒新停浊酒杯。

江汉

江汉思归客，乾坤一腐儒。
片云天共远，永夜月同孤。
落日心犹壮，秋风病欲苏。
古来存老马，不必取长途。

登岳阳楼

昔闻洞庭水，今上岳阳楼。
吴楚东南坼，乾坤日夜浮。
亲朋无一字，老病有孤舟。
戎马关山北，凭轩涕泗流。

江南逢李龟年

岐王宅里寻常见，崔九堂前几度闻。
正是江南好风景，落花时节又逢君。

白雪歌送武判官归京

北风卷地白草折，胡天八月即飞雪。
忽如一夜春风来，千树万树梨花开。
散入珠帘湿罗幕，狐裘不暖锦衾薄。
将军角弓不得控，都护铁衣冷难着。
瀚海阑干百丈冰，愁云惨淡万里凝。
中军置酒饮归客，胡琴琵琶与羌笛。
纷纷暮雪下辕门，风掣红旗冻不翻。
轮台东门送君去，去时雪满天山路。
山回路转不见君，雪上空留马行处。

走马川行奉送出师西征

君不见：走马川，雪海边，
平沙莽莽黄入天。
轮台九月风夜吼，一川碎石大如斗，
随风满地石乱走。
匈奴草黄马正肥，金山西见烟尘飞，
汉家大将西出师。
将军金甲夜不脱，半夜军行戈相拨，
风头如刀面如割。
马毛带雪汗气蒸，五花连钱旋作冰，
幕中草檄砚水凝。
虏骑闻之应胆慑，料知短兵不敢接，
车师西门伫献捷。

山房春事

梁园日暮乱飞鸦，极目萧条三两家。
庭树不知人去尽，春来还发旧时花。

逢入京使

故园东望路漫漫，双袖龙钟泪不干。
马上相逢无纸笔，凭君传语报平安。

春梦

洞房昨夜春风起，遥忆美人湘江水。
枕上片时春梦中，行尽江南数千里。

贾至

春思

草色青青柳色黄，桃花历乱李花香。
东风不为吹愁去，春日偏能惹恨长。

初至巴陵与李十二白裴九同泛洞庭湖

枫岸纷纷落叶多，洞庭秋水晚来波。
乘兴轻舟无近远，白云明月吊湘娥。

石鱼湖上醉歌

石鱼湖，似洞庭，夏水欲满君山青。
山为樽，水为沼，酒徒历历坐洲岛。
长风连日作大浪，不能废人运酒舫。
我持长瓢坐巴丘，酌饮四座以散愁。

月夜

更深月色半人家，北斗阑干南斗斜。
今夜偏知春气暖，虫声新透绿窗纱。

春怨

纱窗日落渐黄昏，金屋无人见泪痕。
寂寞空庭春欲晚，梨花满地不开门。

司空曙

江村即事

钓罢归来不系船，江村月落正堪眠。
纵然一夜风吹去，只在芦花浅水边。

别卢秦卿

知有前期在，难分此夜中。
无将故人酒，不及石尤风。

钱起

归雁

潇湘何事等闲回？水碧沙明两岸苔。
二十五弦弹夜月，不胜清怨却飞来。

顾况

宫词

玉楼天半起笙歌，风送宫嫔笑语和。
月殿影开闻夜漏，水晶帘卷近秋河。

张继

枫桥夜泊

月落乌啼霜满天，江枫渔火对愁眠。
姑苏城外寒山寺，夜半钟声到客船。

韩翃

寒食

春城无处不飞花，寒食东风御柳斜。
日暮汉宫传蜡烛，轻烟散入五侯家。

韦应物

秋夜寄丘二十二员外

怀君属秋夜，散步咏凉天。
空山松子落，幽人应未眠。

滁州西涧

独怜幽草涧边生，上有黄鹂深树鸣。
春潮带雨晚来急，野渡无人舟自横。

耿沣

秋日

反照入闾巷，忧来谁与语？
古道无人行，秋风动禾黍。

卢纶

伤秋

岁去人头白，秋来树叶黄。
搔头向黄叶，与尔共悲伤。

塞下曲

一

鹫翎金仆姑，燕尾绣蝥弧。
独立扬新令，千营共一呼。

二

林暗草惊风，将军夜引弓。
平明寻白羽，没在石棱中。

三

月黑雁飞高，单于夜遁逃。
欲将轻骑逐，大雪满弓刀。

四

野幕敞琼筵，羌戎贺劳旋。
醉和金甲舞，雷鼓动山川。

李益

喜见外弟又言别

十年离乱后，长大一相逢。
问姓惊初见，称名忆旧容。
别来沧海事，语罢暮天钟。
明日巴陵道，秋山又几重。

宫怨

露湿晴花春殿香，月明歌吹在昭阳。
似将海水添宫漏，共滴长门一夜长。

夜上受降城闻笛

回乐峰前沙似雪，受降城外月如霜。
不知何处吹芦管，一夜征人尽望乡。

江南曲

嫁得瞿塘贾，朝朝误妾期。
早知潮有信，嫁与弄潮儿。

李端

鸣筝

鸣筝金粟柱，素手玉房前。
欲得周郎顾，时时误拂弦。

孟郊

游子吟

慈母手中线，游子身上衣。
临行密密缝，意恐迟迟归。
谁言寸草心，报得三春晖？

古别离

欲别牵郎衣，郎今到何处？
不恨归来迟，莫向临邛去！

登科后

昔日龌龊不足夸，今朝放荡思无涯。
春风得意马蹄疾，一日看尽长安花。

移家别湖上亭

好是春风湖上亭，柳条藤蔓系离情。
黄莺久住浑相识，欲别频啼四五声。

江边柳

袅袅古堤边，青青一树烟。
若为丝不断，留取系郎船。

八月十五夜赠张功曹

纤云四卷天无河，清风吹空月舒波。
沙平水息声影绝，一杯相属君当歌。
君歌声酸辞正苦，不能听终泪如雨。
"洞庭连天九疑高，蛟龙出没猩鼯号。
十生九死到官所，幽居默默如藏逃。
下床畏蛇食畏药，海气湿蛰薰腥臊。
昨者州前捶大鼓，嗣皇继圣登夔皋。

赦书一日行万里，罪从大辟皆除死。
迁者追回流者还，涤瑕荡垢清朝班。
州家申名使家抑，坎坷只得移荆蛮。
判司卑官不堪说，未免捶楚尘埃间。
同时辈流多上道，天路幽险难追攀。"
君歌且休听我歌，我歌今与君殊科？
一年明月今宵多，人生由命非由他。
有酒不饮奈明何？

左迁至蓝关示侄孙湘

一封朝奏九重天，夕贬潮州路八千。
欲为圣明除弊事，肯将衰朽惜残年？
云横秦岭家何在？雪拥蓝关马不前。
知汝远来应有意，好收吾骨瘴江边。

早春呈水部张十八员外

天街小雨润如酥，草色遥看近却无。
最是一年春好处，绝胜烟柳满皇都。

节妇吟

君知妾有夫，赠妾双明珠。
感君缠绵意，系在红罗襦。
妾家高楼连苑起，良人执戟明光里。
知君用心如日月，事夫誓拟同生死。
还君明珠双泪垂，恨不相逢未嫁时。

望夫石

望夫处，江悠悠，化为石，不回头。
山头日日风复雨，行人归来石应语。

新嫁娘

三日入厨下，洗手作羹汤。
未谙姑食性，先遣小姑尝。

张仲素

春闺思

袅袅城边柳，青青陌上桑。
提笼忘采叶，昨夜梦渔阳。

燕子楼

一

楼上残灯伴晓霜，独眠人起合欢床。
相思一夜情多少？地角天涯未是长。

二

北邙松柏锁愁烟，燕子楼中思悄然。
自埋剑履歌尘散，红袖香销已十年。

三

适看鸿雁洛阳回，又睹玄禽逼社来。
瑶瑟玉箫无意绪，任从蛛网任从灰。

酬乐天扬州初逢席上见赠

巴山楚水凄凉地，二十三年弃置身。
怀旧空吟闻笛赋，到乡翻似烂柯人。
沉舟侧畔千帆过，病树前头万木春。
今日听君歌一曲，暂凭杯酒长精神。

秋风引

何处秋风至？萧萧送雁群。
朝来入庭树，孤客最先闻。

竹枝词（选三）

一

杨柳青青江水平，闻郎江上唱歌声。
东边日出西边雨，道是无晴还有情。

二

山桃红花满上头，蜀江春水拍山流。
花红易衰似郎意，水流无限似侬愁。

九

山上层层桃李花，云间烟火是人家。
银钏金钗来负水，长刀短笠去烧畲。

石头城

山围故国周遭在，潮打空城寂寞回。
淮水东边旧时月，夜深还过女墙来。

乌衣巷

朱雀桥边野草花，乌衣巷口夕阳斜。
旧时王谢堂前燕，飞入寻常百姓家。

和乐天春词

新妆宜面下朱楼，深锁春光一院愁。
行到中庭数花朵，蜻蜓飞上玉搔头。

望洞庭

湖光秋月两相和，潭面无风镜未磨。
遥望洞庭山水色，白银盘里一青螺。

饮酒看牡丹

今日花前饮，甘心醉数杯。
但愁花有语："不为老人开！"

柳枝词

清江一曲柳千条，二十年前旧板桥。
曾与美人桥上别，恨无消息到今朝。

白居易

买花

帝城春欲暮，喧喧车马度。
共道牡丹时，相随买花去。
贵贱无常价，酬直看花数。
灼灼百朵红，戋戋五束素。
上张幄幕庇，旁织笆篱护。
水洒复泥封，移来色如故。
家家习为俗，人人迷不悟。
有一田舍翁，偶来买花处。
低头独长叹，此叹无人喻。
一丛深色花，十户中人赋。

上阳白发人

上阳人，红颜暗老白发新。

绿衣监使守宫门，一闭上阳多少春！

玄宗末岁初选入，入时十六今六十。

同时采择百余人，零落年深残此身。

忆昔吞悲别亲族，扶入车中不教哭。

皆云入内便承恩，脸似芙蓉胸似玉。

未容君王得见面，已被杨妃遥侧目。

妒令潜配上阳宫，一生遂向空房宿。

宿空房，秋夜长，夜长无寐天不明。

耿耿残灯背壁影，萧萧暗雨打窗声。

春日迟，日迟独坐天难暮。

宫莺百啭愁厌闻，梁燕双栖老休妒。

莺归燕去长悄然，春往秋来不记年。

唯向深宫望明月，东西四五百回圆。

今日宫中年最老，大家遥赐尚书号。

小头鞋履窄衣裳，青黛点眉眉细长。

外人不见见应笑，天宝末年时世妆。

上阳人，苦最多。

少亦苦，老亦苦，

少苦老苦两如何？

君不见：昔时吕向美人赋？

又不见：今日上阳白发歌！

卖炭翁

卖炭翁，伐薪烧炭南山中。
满面尘灰烟火色，两鬓苍苍十指黑。
卖炭得钱何所营？身上衣裳口中食。
可怜身上衣正单，心忧炭贱愿天寒。
夜来城外一尺雪，晓驾炭车辗冰辙。
牛困人饥日已高，市南门外泥中歇。
翩翩两骑来是谁？黄衣使者白衫儿。
手把文书口称敕，回车叱牛牵向北。
一车炭，千余斤，宫使驱将惜不得。
半匹红纱一丈绫，系向牛头充炭直。

长恨歌

汉皇重色思倾国，御宇多年求不得。
杨家有女初长成，养在深闺人未识。
天生丽质难自弃，一朝选在君王侧。
回眸一笑百媚生，六宫粉黛无颜色。
春寒赐浴华清池，温泉水滑洗凝脂，
侍儿扶起娇无力，始是新承恩泽时。
云鬓花颜金步摇，芙蓉帐暖度春宵，
春宵苦短日高起，从此君王不早朝！
承欢侍宴无闲暇，春从春游夜专夜。
后宫佳丽三千人，三千宠爱在一身：
金屋妆成娇侍夜，玉楼宴罢醉和春。

姊妹弟兄皆列土，可怜光彩生门户，
遂令天下父母心，不重生男重生女！
骊宫高处入青云，仙乐风飘处处闻。
缓歌慢舞凝丝竹，尽日君王看不足。
渔阳鼙鼓动地来，惊破《霓裳羽衣曲》！
九重城阙烟尘生，千乘万骑西南行。
翠华摇摇行复止，西出都门百余里，
六军不发无奈何，宛转蛾眉马前死。
花钿委地无人收，翠翘金雀玉搔头，
君王掩面救不得，回看血泪相和流！
黄埃散漫风萧索，云栈萦纡登剑阁。
峨嵋山下少人行，旌旗无光日色薄。
蜀江水碧蜀山青，圣主朝朝暮暮情；
行宫见月伤心色，夜雨闻铃肠断声。
天旋地转回龙驭，到此踌躇不能去，
马嵬坡下泥土中，不见玉颜空死处。
君臣相顾尽沾衣，东望都门信马归。
归来池苑皆依旧，太液芙蓉未央柳；
芙蓉如面柳如眉，对此如何不泪垂！
春风桃李花开日，秋雨梧桐叶落时。
西宫南内多秋草，落叶满阶红不扫；
梨园弟子白发新，椒房阿监青娥老。
夕殿萤飞思悄然，孤灯挑尽未成眠，
迟迟钟鼓初长夜，耿耿星河欲曙天。

鸳鸯瓦冷霜华重，翡翠衾寒谁与共！
悠悠生死别经年，魂魄不曾来入梦。
临邛道士鸿都客，能以精诚致魂魄，
为感君王辗转思，遂教方士殷勤觅。
排空驭气奔如电，升天入地求之遍，
上穷碧落下黄泉，两处茫茫皆不见。
忽闻海上有仙山，山在虚无缥缈间，
楼阁玲珑五云起，其中绰约多仙子。
中有一人字太真，雪肤花貌参差是。
金阙西厢叩玉扃，转教小玉报双成；
闻道汉家天子使，九华帐里梦魂惊。
揽衣推枕起徘徊，珠箔银屏迤逦开，
云鬓半偏新睡觉，花冠不整下堂来。
风吹仙袂飘飘举，犹似《霓裳羽衣》舞。
玉容寂寞泪阑干，梨花一枝春带雨。
含情凝睇谢君王，一别音容两渺茫。
昭阳殿里恩爱绝，蓬莱宫中日月长。
回头下望人寰处，不见长安见尘雾。
惟将旧物表深情，钿合金钗寄将去：
钗留一股合一扇，钗擘黄金合分钿。
但教心似金钿坚，天上人间会相见。
临别殷勤重寄词，词中有誓两心知：
七月七日长生殿，夜半无人私语时，
"在天愿作比翼鸟，在地愿为连理枝。"
天长地久有时尽，此恨绵绵无绝期！

琵琶行

浔阳江头夜送客，枫叶荻花秋瑟瑟，
主人下马客在船，举酒欲饮无管弦。
醉不成欢惨将别，别时茫茫江浸月。
忽闻水上琵琶声，主人忘归客不发。
寻声暗问"弹者谁？"琵琶声停欲语迟。
移船相近邀相见，添酒回灯重开宴，
千呼万唤始出来，犹抱琵琶半遮面。
转轴拨弦三两声，未成曲调先有情，
弦弦掩抑声声思，似诉平生不得志。
低眉信手续续弹，说尽心中无限事。
轻拢慢捻抹复挑，初为《霓裳》后《六幺》。
大弦嘈嘈如急雨，小弦切切如私语；
嘈嘈切切错杂弹，大珠小珠落玉盘。
间关莺语花底滑，幽咽泉流水下滩，
水泉冷涩弦凝绝，凝绝不通声暂歇。
别有幽愁暗恨生，此时无声胜有声。
银瓶乍破水浆迸，铁骑突出刀枪鸣。
曲终收拨当心划，四弦一声如裂帛；
东船西舫悄无言，惟见江心秋月白。
沉吟放拨插弦中，整顿衣裳起敛容。
自言"本是京城女，家在虾蟆陵下住。
十三学得琵琶成，名属教坊第一部。
曲罢曾教善才服，妆成每被秋娘妒。

五陵年少争缠头，一曲红绡不知数。
钿头银篦击节碎，血色罗裙翻酒污。
今年欢笑复明年，秋月春风等闲度。
弟走从军阿姨死，暮去朝来颜色故，
门前冷落车马稀，老大嫁作商人妇。
商人重利轻别离，前月浮梁买茶去。
去来江口守空船，绕船月明江水寒，
夜深忽梦少年事，梦啼妆泪红阑干。"
我闻琵琶已叹息，又闻此语重唧唧，
同是天涯沦落人，相逢何必曾相识！
"我从去年辞帝京，谪居卧病浔阳城，
浔阳地僻无音乐，终岁不闻丝竹声。
住近湓江地低湿，黄芦苦竹绕宅生。
其间旦暮闻何物？杜鹃啼血猿哀鸣。
春江花朝秋月夜，往往取酒还独倾，
岂无山歌与村笛？呕哑嘲哳难为听。
今夜闻君琵琶语，如听仙乐耳暂明。
莫辞更坐弹一曲，为君翻作《琵琶行》。"
感我此言良久立，却坐促弦弦转急，
凄凄不似向前声，满座重闻皆掩泣。
座中泣下谁最多？江州司马青衫湿！

花非花

花非花，雾非雾。
夜半来，天明去。
来如春梦几多时？
去似朝云无觅处。

赋得古原草送别

离离原上草，一岁一枯荣。
野火烧不尽，春风吹又生。
远芳侵古道，晴翠接荒城。
又送王孙去，萋萋满别情。

惜牡丹花

惆怅阶前红牡丹，晚来唯有两枝残。
明朝风起应吹尽，夜惜衰红把火看。

燕子楼

一

满窗明月满帘霜，被冷灯残拂卧床。
燕子楼中霜月夜，秋来只为一人长。

二

钿晕罗衫色似烟，几回欲著即潸然。
自从不舞霓裳曲，叠在空箱十一年。

三

今春有客洛阳回，曾到尚书墓上来。
见说白杨堪作柱，争教红粉不成灰？

大林寺桃花

人间四月芳菲尽，山寺桃花始盛开。
长恨春归无觅处，不知转入此中来。

问刘十九

绿蚁新醅酒，红泥小火炉。
晚来天欲雪，能饮一杯无？

后宫词

泪湿罗巾梦不成，夜深前殿按歌声。
红颜未老恩先断，斜倚熏笼坐到明。

暮江吟

一道残阳铺水中，半江瑟瑟半江红。
可怜九月初三夜，露似真珠月似弓。

钱塘湖春行

孤山寺北贾亭西，水面初平云脚低。
几处早莺争暖树？谁家新燕啄春泥？
乱花渐欲迷人眼，浅草才能没马蹄。
最爱湖东行不足，绿杨阴里白沙堤。

白云泉

天平山上白云泉，云自无心水自闲。
何必奔冲山下去？更添波浪向人间！

红鹦鹉

安南远进红鹦鹉，色似桃花语似人。
文章辩慧皆如此，笼槛何年出得身？

昼卧

抱枕无言语，空房独悄然。
谁知尽日卧，非病亦非眠？

病中

交亲不要苦相忧，亦拟时时强出游。
但有心情何用脚？陆乘肩舆水乘舟。

羊士谔

登楼

槐柳萧疏绕郡城，夜添山雨作江声。
秋风南陌无车马，独上高楼故国情。

刘皂

旅次朔方

客舍并州已十霜，归心日夜忆咸阳。
无端又渡桑干水，却望并州是故乡。

柳宗元

登柳州城楼寄漳汀封连四州刺史

城上高楼接大荒，海天愁思正茫茫。
惊风乱飐芙蓉水，密雨斜侵薜荔墙。
岭树重遮千里目，江流曲似九回肠。
共来百粤文身地，犹自音书滞一乡。

江雪

千山鸟飞绝，万径人踪灭。
孤舟蓑笠翁，独钓寒江雪。

渔翁

渔翁夜傍西岩宿，晓汲清湘燃楚竹。
烟销日出不见人，欸乃一声山水绿。
回看天际下中流，岩上无心云相逐。

饮酒

今旦少愉乐，起坐开清樽。
举觞酹先酒，为我驱忧烦。
须臾心自殊，顿觉天地喧。
连山变幽晦，绿水函晏温。
蔼蔼南郭门，树木一何繁！
清阴可自庇，竟夕闻佳言。
尽醉无复辞，偃卧有芳荪。
彼哉晋楚富，此道未必存。

崔护

题都城南庄

去年今日此门中，人面桃花相映红。
人面不知何处去，桃花依旧笑春风。

元稹

遣悲怀

一

谢公最小偏怜女，自嫁黔娄百事乖。
顾我无衣搜荩箧，泥他沽酒拔金钗。
野蔬充膳甘长藿，落叶添薪仰古槐。
今日俸钱过十万，与君营奠复营斋。

二

昔日戏言身后意，今朝都到眼前来。
衣裳已施行看尽，针线犹存未忍开。
尚想旧情怜婢仆，也曾因梦送钱财。
诚知此恨人人有，贫贱夫妻百事哀。

三

闲坐悲君亦自悲，百年都是几多时？
邓攸无子寻知命，潘岳悼亡犹费词。
同穴窅冥何所望？他生缘会更难期！
惟将终夜长开眼，报答平生未展眉。

行宫

寥落古行宫，宫花寂寞红。
白头宫女在，闲坐说玄宗。

菊花

秋丛绕舍似陶家，遍绕篱边日渐斜。
不是花中偏爱菊，此花开尽更无花。

离思

曾经沧海难为水，除却巫山不是云。
取次花丛懒回顾，半缘修道半缘君。

贾岛

剑客

十年磨一剑，霜刃未曾试。
今日把示君，谁有不平事？

题兴化寺园亭

破却千家作一池，不栽桃李种蔷薇。
蔷薇花落秋风起，荆棘满亭君自知。

访隐者不遇

松下问童子，言师采药去。
只在此山中，云深不知处。

李绅

悯农二首

一

春种一粒粟，秋收万颗子。
四海无闲田，农夫犹饿死。

二

锄禾日当午，汗滴禾下土。
谁知盘中餐，粒粒皆辛苦！

春望词

一

花开不同赏，花落不同悲。
欲问相思处，花开花落时。

二

揽草结同心，将以遗知音。
春愁正断绝，春鸟复哀吟。

三

风花日将老，佳期犹渺渺。
不结同心人，空结同心草。

四

那堪花满枝，翻作两相思？
玉箸垂朝镜，春风知不知？

酬人雨后玩竹

南天春雨时，那鉴雪霜姿？
众类亦云茂，虚心能自持。
多留晋贤醉，早伴舜妃悲。
晚岁君能赏，苍苍劲节奇。

寄旧诗与元微之

诗篇调态人皆有，细腻风光我独知。
月夜吟花怜暗淡，雨朝题柳为欹垂。
长教碧玉藏深处，总向红笺写自随。
老大不能收拾得，与君开似好男儿。

张祜

何满子

故国三千里，深宫二十年。
一声何满子，双泪落君前。

赠内人

禁门宫树月痕过，媚眼惟看宿鹭窠。
斜拔玉钗灯影畔，剔开红焰救飞蛾。

集灵台

虢国夫人承主恩，平明骑马入宫门。
却嫌脂粉污颜色，淡扫蛾眉朝至尊。

题金陵渡

金陵津渡小山楼，一宿行人自可愁。
潮落夜江斜月里，两三星火是瓜洲。

李涉

再宿武关

远别秦城万里游，乱山高下出商州。
关门不锁寒溪水，一夜潺湲送客愁。

崔郊

赠婢

公子王孙逐后尘，绿珠垂泪滴罗巾。
侯门一入深如海，从此萧郎是路人。

李贺

雁门太守行

黑云压城城欲摧，甲光向日金鳞开。
角声满天秋色里，塞上燕脂凝夜紫。
半卷红旗临易水，霜重鼓寒声不起。
报君黄金台上意，提携玉龙为君死。

苏小小墓

幽兰露，如啼眼。
无物结同心，烟花不堪剪。
草如茵，松如盖。风为裳，水为佩。
油壁车，久相待。冷翠烛，劳光彩。
西陵下，风吹雨。

梦天

老兔寒蟾泣天色，云楼半开壁斜白。
玉轮轧露湿团光，鸾佩相逢桂香陌。
黄尘清水三山下，更变千年如走马。
遥望齐州九点烟，一泓海水杯中泻。

天上谣

天河夜转漂回星，银浦流云学水声。
玉宫桂树花未落，仙妾采香垂佩缨。
秦妃卷帘北窗晓，窗前植桐青凤小；
王子吹笙鹅管长，呼龙耕烟种瑶草。
粉霞红绶藕丝裙，青洲步拾兰苕春。
东指羲和能走马，海尘新生石山下。

浩歌

南风吹山作平地，帝遣天吴移海水。
王母桃花千遍红，彭祖巫咸几回死？
青毛骢马参差钱，娇春杨柳含细烟。
筝人劝我金屈卮，神血未凝身问谁？
不需浪饮丁都护，世上英雄本无主。
买丝绣作平原君，有酒唯浇赵州土。
漏催水咽玉蟾蜍，卫娘发薄不胜梳。
看见秋眉换新绿，二十男儿那刺促？

秋来

桐风惊心壮士苦，衰灯络纬啼寒素。
谁看青简一编书，不遣花虫粉空蠹？
思牵今夜肠应直，雨冷香魂吊书客。
秋魂鬼唱鲍家诗，恨血千年土中碧。

秦王饮酒

秦王骑虎游八极，剑光照空天自碧。
羲和敲日玻璃声，劫灰飞尽古今平。
龙头泻酒邀酒星，金槽琵琶夜枨枨。
洞庭雨脚来吹笙，酒酣喝月使倒行。
银云栉栉瑶殿明，宫门掌事报一更。
花楼玉凤声娇狞，海绡红文香浅清，
黄娥跌舞千年觥。
仙人烛树蜡烟轻，青琴醉眼泪泓泓。

南园

其一

花枝草蔓眼中开，小白长红越女腮。
可怜日暮嫣香落，嫁与东风不用媒。

其五

男儿何不带吴钩，收取关山五十州？
请君暂上凌烟阁，若个书生万户侯？

其六

寻章摘句老雕虫，晓月当帘挂玉弓。
不见年年辽海上，文章何处哭秋风？

其七

长卿牢落悲空合，曼倩诙谐取自容。
见买若耶溪水剑，明朝归去事猿公。

其八

春水初生乳燕飞，黄蜂小尾扑花归。
窗含远色通书幌，鱼拥香钩近石矶。

金铜仙人辞汉歌并序

魏明帝青龙元年八月，诏宫官牵车西取汉孝武捧露盘仙人，欲立置前殿。宫官既拆盘，仙人临载，乃潸然泪下，唐诸王孙李长吉遂作《金铜仙人辞汉歌》。

茂陵刘郎秋风客，夜闻马嘶晓无迹。
画栏桂树悬秋香，三十六宫土花碧。
魏官牵车指千里，东关酸风射眸子。
空将汉月出宫门，忆君清泪如铅水。
衰兰送客咸阳道，天若有情天亦老。
携盘独出月荒凉，渭城已远波声小。

马诗二十三首（选四）

一

龙背贴连钱，银蹄白踏烟。
无人织绵韂，谁为铸金鞭。

四

此马非凡马，房星本是星。
向前敲瘦骨，犹自带铜声。

五

大漠沙如雪，燕山月似钩。
何当金络脑，快走踏清秋？

二十三

武帝爱神仙，烧金得紫烟。
厩中皆肉马，不解上青天！

神弦曲

西山日没东山昏，旋风吹马马踏云。
画弦素管声浅繁，花裙缀繺步秋尘，
桂叶刷风桂坠子，青狸哭血寒狐死。
古壁彩虬金帖尾，雨工骑入秋潭水。
百年老鸮成木魅，笑声碧火巢中起。

将进酒

琉璃钟，琥珀浓，小槽酒滴真珠红。
烹龙炮凤玉脂泣，罗帏绣幕围香风。
吹龙笛，击鼍鼓；皓齿歌，细腰舞。
况是青春日将暮，桃花乱落如红雨，
劝君终日酩酊醉，酒不到刘伶坟上土！

官街鼓

晓声隆隆催转日，暮声隆隆呼月出。
汉城黄柳映新帘，柏陵飞燕埋香骨。
槌碎千年日长白，孝武秦王听不得。
从君翠发芦花色，独共南山守中国。
几回天上葬神仙，漏声相将无断绝。

许浑

咸阳城西楼晚眺

一上高城万里愁，蒹葭杨柳似汀洲。
溪云初起日沉阁，山雨欲来风满楼。
鸟下绿芜秦苑夕，蝉鸣黄叶汉宫秋。
行人莫问当年事，故国东来渭水流。

塞下曲

夜战桑干北，秦兵半不归。
朝来有乡信，犹自寄寒衣。

谢亭送别

劳歌一曲解行舟，红叶青山水急流。
日暮酒醒人已远，满天风雨下西楼。

忆扬州

萧娘脸薄难胜泪，桃叶眉长易觉愁。
天下三分明月夜，二分无赖是扬州。

过华清宫

长安回望绣成堆，山顶千门次第开。
一骑红尘妃子笑，无人知是荔枝来。

沈下贤

斯人清唱何人和？草径苔芜不可寻。
一夕小敷山下梦，水如环佩月如襟。

将赴宜兴登乐游原一绝

清时有味是无能，闲爱孤云静爱僧。
欲把一麾江海去，乐游原上望昭陵。

题扬州禅智寺

雨过一蝉噪，飘萧松桂秋。
青苔满阶砌，白鸟故迟留。
暮霭生深树，斜阳下小楼。
谁知竹西路，歌吹是扬州？

江南春

千里莺啼绿映红，水村山郭酒旗风。
南朝四百八十寺，多少楼台烟雨中。

题宣州开元寺水阁，阁下宛溪，夹溪居人

六朝文物草连空，天淡云闲今古同。
鸟去鸟来山色里，人歌人哭水声中。
深秋帘幕千家雨，落日楼台一笛风。
惆怅无因见范蠡，参差烟树五湖东。

登九峰楼寄张祜

百感衷来不自由，角声孤起夕阳楼，
碧山终日思无尽，芳草何年恨即休？
睫在眼前长不见，道非身外更何求？
谁人得似张公子，千首诗轻万户侯？

九日齐山登高

江涵秋影雁初飞，与客携壶上翠微，
尘世难逢开口笑，菊花须插满头归。
但将酩酊酬佳节，不用登临恨落晖。
古往今来只如此，牛山何必独沾衣！

齐安郡中偶题

两竿落日溪桥上，半缕轻烟柳影中。
多少绿荷相倚恨，一时回首背西风。

惜春

春半年已除，其余强为有。
即此醉残花，便同尝腊酒。
怅望送春杯，殷勤扫花帚。
谁为驻东流？年年长在手。

赤壁

折戟沉沙铁未销，自将磨洗认前朝。
东风不与周郎便，铜雀春深锁二乔。

泊秦淮

烟笼寒水月笼沙，夜泊秦淮近酒家。
商女不知亡国恨，隔江犹唱后庭花。

赠别

一

娉娉袅袅十三余，豆蔻梢头二月初。
春风十里扬州路，卷上珠帘总不如。

二

多情却似总无情，唯觉樽前笑不成。
蜡烛有心还惜别，替人垂泪到天明。

遣怀

落魄江湖载酒行，楚腰纤细掌中轻。
十年一觉扬州梦，赢得青楼薄倖名。

山行

远上寒山石径斜，白云生处有人家。
停车坐爱枫林晚，霜叶红于二月花。

秋夕

银烛秋光冷画屏，轻罗小扇扑流萤。
天阶夜色凉如水，卧看牵牛织女星。

金谷园

繁华事散逐香尘，流水无情草自春。
日暮东风怨啼鸟，落花犹似坠楼人。

清明

清明时节雨纷纷，路上行人欲断魂。
借问酒家何处有？牧童遥指杏花村。

雍陶

题情尽桥

从来只有情难尽，何事名为情尽桥？
自此改名为折柳，任他离恨一条条！

朱庆余

宫中词

寂寂花时闭院门，美人相并立琼轩。
含情欲说宫中事，鹦鹉前头不敢言。

近试上张水部

洞房昨夜停红烛，待晓堂前拜舅姑。
妆罢低声问夫婿，画眉深浅入时无？

过分水岭

溪水无情似有情，入山三日得同行。
岭头便是分头处，惜别潺湲一夜声。

嘲三月十八日雪

三月雪连夜，未应伤物华。
只缘春欲尽，留着伴梨花。

商山早行

晨起动征铎，客行悲故乡。
鸡声茅店月，人迹板桥霜。
槲叶落山路，枳花明驿墙。
因思杜陵梦，凫雁满回塘。

锦瑟

锦瑟无端五十弦，一弦一柱思华年。
庄生晓梦迷蝴蝶，望帝春心托杜鹃。
沧海月明珠有泪，蓝田日暖玉生烟。
此情可待成追忆？只是当时已惘然。

重过圣女祠

白石岩扉碧藓滋，上清沦谪得归迟。
一春梦雨常飘瓦，尽日灵风不满旗。
萼绿华来无定所，杜兰香去未移时。
玉郎会此通仙籍，忆向天阶问紫芝。

赠刘司户蒉

江风扬浪动云根，重碇危樯白日昏。
已断燕鸿初起势，更惊骚客后归魂。
汉廷急诏谁先入？楚路高歌意欲翻。
万里相逢欢复泣，凤巢西隔九重门。

乐游原

向晚意不适，驱车登古原。
夕阳无限好，只是近黄昏。

北齐二首

其一

一笑相倾国便亡，何劳荆棘始堪伤？
小怜玉体横陈夜，已报周师入晋阳。

其二

巧笑知堪敌万机，倾城最在著戎衣。
晋阳已陷休回顾，更请君王猎一回。

夜雨寄北

君问归期未有期，巴山夜雨涨秋池。
何当共剪西窗烛？却话巴山夜雨时。

风雨

凄凉宝剑篇，羁泊欲穷年。
黄叶仍风雨，青楼自管弦。
新知遭薄俗，旧好隔良缘。
心断新丰酒，销愁斗几千！

寄令狐郎中

嵩云秦树久离居，双鲤迢迢一纸书。
休问梁园旧宾客，茂陵秋雨病相如。

哭刘蕡

上帝深宫闭九阍，巫咸不下问衔冤。
黄陵别后春涛隔，溢浦书来秋雨翻。
只有安仁能作诔，何曾宋玉解招魂？
平生风义兼师友，不敢同君哭寝门。

杜司勋

高楼风雨感斯文，短翼差池不及群。
刻意伤春复伤别，人间唯有杜司勋。

杜工部蜀中离席

人生何处不离群？世路干戈惜暂分，
雪岭未归天外使，松州犹驻殿前军。
座中醉客延醒客，江上晴云杂雨云。
美酒成都堪送老，当垆仍是卓文君。

隋宫

紫泉宫殿锁烟霞，欲取芜城作帝家。
玉玺不缘归日角，锦帆应是到天涯。
于今腐草无萤火，终古垂杨有暮鸦。
地下若逢陈后主，岂宜重问《后庭花》？

二月二日

二月二日江上行，东风日暖闻吹笙。
花须柳眼各无赖，紫蝶黄蜂俱有情。
万里忆归元亮井，三年从事亚夫营。
新滩莫悟游人意，更作风檐雨夜声。

筹笔驿

猿鸟犹疑畏简书，风云长为护储胥。
徒令上将挥神笔，终见降王走传车。
管乐有才真不忝，关张无命欲何如？
他年锦里经祠庙，梁父吟成恨有余。

无题

昨夜星辰昨夜风，画楼西畔桂堂东。
身无彩凤双飞翼，心有灵犀一点通。
隔座送钩春酒暖，分曹射覆蜡灯红。
嗟余听鼓应官去，走马兰台类转蓬。

无题四首（选三）

一

来是空言去绝踪，月斜楼上五更钟。
梦为远别啼难唤，书被催成墨未浓。
蜡照半笼金翡翠，麝熏微度绣芙蓉。
刘郎已恨蓬山远，更隔蓬山一万重。

二

飒飒东风细雨来，芙蓉塘外有轻雷。
金蟾啮锁烧香入，玉虎牵丝汲井回。
贾氏窥帘韩掾少，宓妃留枕魏王才。
春心莫共花争发，一寸相思一寸灰。

四

何处哀筝随急管？樱花永巷垂杨岸。
东家老女嫁不售，白日当天三月半。
溧阳公主年十四，清明暖后同墙看。
归来展转到五更，梁间燕子闻长叹。

隋宫（二）

乘兴南游不戒严，九重谁省谏书函？
春风举国裁宫锦，半作障泥半作帆。

柳

曾逐东风拂舞筵，乐游春苑断肠天。
如何肯到清秋日，已带斜阳又带蝉！

无题

相见时难别亦难，东风无力百花残。
春蚕到死丝方尽，蜡炬成灰泪始干。
晓镜但愁云鬓改，夜吟应觉月光寒。
蓬山此去无多路，青鸟殷勤为探看。

碧城

碧城十二曲阑干，犀辟尘埃玉辟寒。
阆苑有书多附鹤，女床无树不栖鸾。
星沉海底当窗见，雨过河源隔座看。
若是晓珠明又定，一生长对水精盘。

齐宫词

永寿兵来夜不扃，金莲无复印中庭。
梁台歌管三更罢，犹自风摇九子铃。

汉宫词

青雀西飞竟未回，君王长在集灵台。
侍臣最有相如渴，不赐金茎露一杯。

离亭赋得折杨柳

一

暂凭尊酒送无憀，莫损愁眉与细腰。
人世死前惟有别，春风争拟惜长条？

二

含烟惹雾每依依，万绪千条拂落晖。
为报行人休尽折，半留相送半迎归。

宫妓

珠箔轻明拂玉墀，披香新殿斗腰支。
不须看尽鱼龙戏，终遣君王怒偃师。

宫辞

君恩如水向东流，得宠忧移失宠愁。
莫向樽前奏花落，凉风只在殿西头。

代赠

楼上黄昏欲望休，玉梯横绝月如钩。
芭蕉不展丁香结，同向春风各自愁。

楚吟

山上高宫宫上楼，楼前宫畔暮江流。
楚天长短黄昏雨，宋玉无愁亦自愁。

板桥晓别

回望高城落晓河，长亭窗户压微波。
水仙欲上鲤鱼去，一夜芙蓉红泪多。

银河吹笙

怅望银河吹玉笙，楼寒院冷接平明。
重衾幽梦他年断，别树羁雌昨夜惊。
月榭故香因雨发，风帘残烛隔霜清。
不须浪作缑山意，湘瑟秦箫自有情。

春雨

怅卧新春白袷衣，白门寥落意多违。
红楼隔雨相望冷，珠箔飘灯独自归。
远路应悲春晼晚，残宵犹得梦依稀。
玉珰缄札何由达？万里云罗一雁飞。

晚晴

深居俯夹城，春去夏犹清。
天意怜幽草，人间重晚晴。
并添高阁迥，微注小窗明。
越鸟巢干后，归飞体更轻。

安定城楼

迢递高城百尺楼，绿杨枝外尽汀洲。
贾生年少虚垂涕，王粲春来更远游。
永忆江湖归白发，欲回天地入扁舟。
不知腐鼠成滋味，猜意鹓雏竟未休。

天涯

春日在天涯，天涯日又斜。
莺啼如有泪，为湿最高花！

日日

日日春光斗日光，山城斜路杏花香。
几时心绪浑无事，得及游丝百尺长？

龙池

龙池赐酒敞云屏，羯鼓声高众乐停。
夜半宴归宫漏永，薛王沉醉寿王醒。
（注）唐玄宗夺寿王妻，封为杨贵妃。

流莺

流莺漂荡复参差，度陌临流不自持。
巧啭岂能无本意？良辰未必有佳期。
风朝露夜阴晴里，万户千门开闭时。
曾苦伤春不忍听，凤城何处有花枝？

嫦娥

云母屏风烛影深，长河渐落晓星沉。
嫦娥应悔偷灵药，碧海青天夜夜心。

无题二首

一

凤尾香罗薄几重？碧文圆顶夜深缝。
扇裁月魄羞难掩，车走雷声语未通。
曾是寂寥金烬暗，断无消息石榴红。
斑骓只系垂杨岸，何处西南待好风？

二

重帏深下莫愁堂，卧后清宵细细长。
神女生涯原是梦，小姑居处本无郎。
风波不信菱枝弱，月露谁教桂叶香？
直道相思了无益，未妨惆怅是清狂。

贾生

宣室求贤访逐臣，贾生才调更无伦。
可怜夜半虚前席，不问苍生问鬼神。

陈陶

陇西行

誓扫匈奴不顾身，五千貂锦丧胡尘。
可怜无定河边骨，犹是春闺梦里人。

李群玉

赠人

曾留宋玉旧衣裳，惹得巫山梦里香。
云雨无情难管领，任他别嫁楚襄王。

官仓鼠

官仓老鼠大如斗，见人开仓亦不走。
健儿无粮百姓饥，谁遣朝朝入君口？

江楼感旧

独上江楼思渺然，月光如水水如天。
同来望月人何处？风景依稀似去年。

哭李商隐

虚负凌云万丈才，一生襟抱未曾开。
鸟啼花落人何在？竹死桐枯凤不来。
良马足因无主踠，旧交心为绝弦哀。
九泉莫叹三光隔，又送文星入夜台。

赠妓云英

钟陵醉别十余春，重见云英掌上身。
我未成名君未嫁，可能俱是不如人。

自遣

得即高歌失即休，多愁多恨亦悠悠。
今朝有酒今朝醉，明日愁来明日愁。

鹦鹉

莫恨雕笼翠羽残，江西地暖陇西寒。
劝君不必分明语，语得分明出转难。

雪

尽道丰年瑞，丰年事若何？
长安有贫者，为瑞不宜多。

韦庄

忆昔

昔年曾向五陵游，子夜歌清月满楼。
银烛树前长似昼，露桃花里不知秋。
西园公子名无忌，南国佳人号莫愁。
今日乱离俱是梦，夕阳唯见水东流。

台城

江雨霏霏江草齐，六朝如梦鸟空啼。
无情最是台城柳，依旧烟笼十里堤。

聂夷中

田家

父耕原上田，子劚山下荒。
六月禾未秀，官家已修仓。

章碣

焚书坑

竹帛烟销帝业虚，关河空锁祖龙居。
坑灰未冷山东乱，刘项元来不读书。

曹松

己亥岁

泽国江山入战图，生民何计乐樵苏？
凭君莫话封侯事，一将功成万骨枯！

韩偓

效崔国辅体

淡月照中庭，海棠花自落。
独立俯闲阶，风动秋千索。

杜荀鹤

山中寡妇

夫因兵死守蓬茅，麻苎衣衫鬓发焦。
桑柘废来犹纳税，田园荒后尚征苗。
时挑野菜和根煮，旋斫生柴带叶烧。
任是深山更深处，也应无计避征徭。

黄巢

题菊花

飒飒西风满院栽，蕊寒香冷蝶难来。
他年我若为青帝，报与桃花一处开。

菊花

待到秋来九月八，我花开后百花杀。
冲天香阵透长安，满城尽带黄金甲。

社日

鹅湖山下稻粱肥，豚栅鸡栖半掩扉。
桑柘影斜春社散，家家扶得醉人归。

雨晴

雨前初见花间蕊，雨后全无叶底花。
蜂蝶纷纷过墙去，却疑春色在邻家。

春闺

欲剪宜春字，春寒入剪刀。
辽阳在何处？莫望寄征袍！

贫女

蓬门未识绮罗香，拟托良媒益自伤。
谁爱风流高格调？共怜时世俭梳妆。
敢将十指夸针巧，不把双眉斗画长。
苦恨年年压金线，为他人作嫁衣裳。

于武陵

赠卖松人

入市虽求利，怜君意独真。
欲将寒涧树，卖与翠楼人。
瘦叶几经雪，淡花应少春。
长安重桃李，徒染六街尘。

皮日休

橡媪叹

秋深橡子熟，散落榛芜冈。
伛偻黄发媪，拾之践晨霜。
移时始盈掬，尽日方满筐。
几曝复几蒸，用作三冬粮。
山前有熟稻，紫穗袭人香。
细获又精存，粒粒如玉珰。
持之纳于官，私家无仓箱。
如何一石余，只作五斗量！
狡吏不畏刑，贪官不避赃。
农时作私债，农毕归官仓。
自冬及于春，橡实诳饥肠。
吾闻田成子，诈仁犹自王。
吁嗟逢橡媪，不觉泪沾裳。

张泌

寄人

别梦依依到谢家，小廊回合曲阑斜。
多情只有春庭月，犹为离人照落花。

无名氏

金缕衣

劝君莫惜金缕衣，劝君须惜少年时。
有花堪折直须折，莫待无花空折枝！

THEORY ON LITERARY TRANSLATION OF THE CHINESE SCHOOL

The theory on literary translation of the Chinese school owes its origin to traditional Chinese culture, including the Confucian and the Taoist school of thought respectively represented by *Thus Spoke the Master* and *Laws Divine and Human.*

It is said in the first chapter of *Laws Divine and Human* that truth can be known, but it may not be the truth you know, and that things may be named, but names are not the things. When applied to literary translation, this may mean that the theory on literary translation can be known, but it may not the unproven theory on the one hand, nor the scientific theory on the other, for neither literary translation nor its theory is science. As the names are not equal to the things, the translation cannot be equal to the original. As there is more difference than equivalence between the Chinese and the English language, the principle of equivalence can not be applied to the translation between them as between two occidental languages.

It is said in the last chapter of *Laws Divine and Human* that truthful words may not be beautiful and beautiful words may not be truthful. That is to say, there is contradiction between truth and beauty or between equivalence and excellence. A translation where equivalents are used may be called a faithful or truthful translation. When no equivalent can be found between two languages, the translator should make use of the best expressions or excellent expressions of the target language. That may be called theory of excellence.

In *Thus Spoke the Master*, Confucius said, "At seventy, I can do what I will without going beyond what is right." Professor Zhu Guangqian said that this has shown the mature state of an artist. I think it may also show the mature state of a literary translator. The literal translator has used the equivalents without going beyond the original in sound; the liberal translator has described the image without going beyond the original in sense; the literary translator has described the scene without going beyond reality. Not to go beyond the original is to be truthful or faithful, and the translator has reached the ordinary level of translation. To do what one will without going beyond the original is not only to be faithful but also to make his translation beautiful, in that case the translator has attained a higher level. To excel the original without going beyond the reality it describes is to attain the highest level.

What is literary translation? It is an art of solving the contradiction between faithfulness (or truth) and beauty. How to solve it? There are three methods, namely, equalization, generalization and particularization. When there is little or no contradition between truth and beauty, equalization or equivalents may be used. When there is contradction between them, generalization may be used to make the meaning clear, and particularization to make a deeper impression.

Confucius said in *Thus Spoke the Master* that it would be good to be understandable, better to be enjoyable and best to be delectable or delightful. When applied to literary translation, this principle means that an understandable translation is good, an enjoyable one is better and a delightful one is best. The ontology or theory of contradition between truth and beauty, the methodology or theory of equalization, generalization and particularization, and the teleology or theory of the understandable, the enjoyable and the delectable, all owe their origin to the Confucian and Taoist schools of thoughts.

But Confucius said less about what delight is and more about how to be delightful. In the beginning of *Thus Spoke the Master* he said it is delightful to acquire knowledge and put it into practice; In Chapter Six he told us how Yan Hui could find delight in reading though living in a humble lane with only a handful of rice to eat and a gourdful of water to drink; In Chapter Eleven, Zeng Xi told us his delight in an spring excursion. From these examples we can see Confucius' theory on delight or teleology, and his theory on practice or methodology. His theory is not scientific but artistic. Since literary translation is an art but not a branch of science, his theory can not only be applied to the practice but also to the theory of literary translation. As his theory has stood the test of time, it is as durable as scientific theories. A theorist on science who studies truth and the truthful should not go beyond what is truthful. A theorist on art or an artist who studies beauty and the beautiful may go beyond what is truthful and faithful.

The contradiction between truth and beauty in Chinese theory on literary translation has developed into a contradiction between equivalence and excellence. As Keats said, "Beauty is truth, truth beauty," we may even say beauty is a virtue, a kind of excellence. When we cannot find the equivalent, we may resort to generalization or particularization.

In short, literary translation is an art to create the beautiful. This is the epistemology of the Chinese school. The contradition between truth and beauty or between equivalence and excellence is its ontology; the theory on equalization, generalization and particularization is its triple methodology; and the theory of the understandable, the enjoyable and the delectable or delightful is its triple teleology.

Xu Yuanchong

Oct. 2011

代后记：中国学派的文学翻译理论

中国学派的文学翻译理论源自中国的传统文化，主要包括儒家思想和道家思想，儒家思想的代表著作是《论语》，道家思想的代表著作是《老子道德经》。

《老子道德经》第一章开始就说："道可道，非常道；名可名，非常名。"联系到翻译理论上来，就是说：翻译理论是可以知道的，是可以说得出来的，但不是只说得出来而经不起实践检验的空头理论，这就是中国学派翻译理论中的实践论。其次，文学翻译理论不能算科学理论（自然科学），与其说是社会科学理论，不如说是人文学科或艺术理论，这就是文学翻译的艺术论，也可以说是相对论。后六个字"名可名，非常名"应用到文学翻译理论上来，可以有两层意思：第一层是原文的文字是描写现实的，但并不等于现实，文字和现实之间还有距离，还有矛盾；第二层意思是译文和原文之间也有距离，也有矛盾，译文和原文所描写的现实之间，自然还有距离，还有矛盾。译文应该发挥译语优势，运用最好的译语表达方式，来和原文展开竞赛，使译文和现实的距离或矛盾小于原文和现实之间的矛盾，那就是超越原文了。这就是文学翻译理论中的优势论或优化论，超越论或竞赛论。文学翻译理论应该解决的不只是译文和原文在文字方面的矛盾，还要解决译文和原文所反映的现实之间的矛盾，这是文学翻译的本体论。

一般翻译只要解决"真"或"信"或"似"的问题，文学翻译却要解决"真"或"信"和"美"之间的矛盾。原文反映的现实不只是言内之意，还有言外之意。中国的文学语言往往有言外之意，甚至还有言外之情。文学翻译理论也要解决译文和原文的言外之意、言外之情的矛盾。

《论语》说："知之者不如好之者，好之者不如乐之者。"知之，好之，乐之，这"三之论"是对艺术论的进一步说明。艺术论第一条原则要求译文忠实于原文所反映的现实，求的是真，可以使人知之；第二条原则要求用"三化"法来优化译文，求的是美，可以使人好之；第三条原则要求用"三美"来优化译文，尤其是译诗词，求的是意美、音美和形美，可以使人乐之。如果"不逾矩"的等化译文能使人知之（理解），那就达到了文学翻译的低标准，如从心所欲而不逾矩的浅化或深化的译文既能使人知之，又能使人好之（喜欢），那就达到了中标准；如果从心所欲的译文不但能使人知之，好之，还能使人乐之（愉快），那才达到了文学翻译的高标准。这也是中国译者对世界译论作出的贡献。

翻译艺术的规律是从心所欲而不逾矩。"矩"就是规矩，规律。但艺术规律却可以依人的主观意志而转移，是因为得到承认才算正确的。所以贝多芬说：为了更美，没有什么清规戒律不可打破。他所说的戒律不是科学规律，而是艺术规律。不能用科学规律来评论文学翻译。

孔子不大谈"什么是"（What?）而多谈"怎么做"（How?）。这是中国传统的方法论，比西方流传更久，影响更广，作用更大，并且经过了两三千年实践的考验。《论语》第一章中说："学而时习之，不亦说（悦，乐）乎！""学"是取得知识，"习"是实践。孔子只说学习实践可以得到乐趣，却不说什么是"乐"。这就是孔子的方法论，是中国文学翻译理论的依据。

总而言之，中国学派的文学翻译理论是研究老子提出的

"信"（似）"美"（优）矛盾的艺术（本体论），但"信"不限原文，还指原文所反映的现实，这是认识论，"信"由严复提出的"信达雅"发展到鲁迅提出"信顺"的直译，再发展到陈源的"三似"（形似，意似，神似），直到傅雷的"重神似不重形似"，这已经接近"美"了。"美"发展到鲁迅的"三美"（意美，音美，形美），再发展到林语堂提出的"忠实，通顺，美"，转化为朱生豪"传达原作意趣"的意译，直到茅盾提出的"美的享受"。孔子提出的"从心所欲"发展到郭沫若提出的创译论（好的翻译等于创作），以及钱钟书说的译文可以胜过原作的"化境"说，再发展到优化论，超越论，"三化"（等化，浅化，深化）方法论。孔子提出的"不逾矩"和老子说的"信言不美，美言不信"有同有异。老子"信美"并重，孔子"从心所欲"重于"不逾矩"，发展为朱光潜的"艺术论"，包括郭沫若说的"在信达之外，愈雅愈好。所谓'雅'不是高深或讲修饰，而是文学价值或艺术价值比较高。"直到茅盾说的："必须把文学翻译工作提高到艺术创造的水平。"孔子的"乐之"发展为胡适之的"愉快"说（翻译要使读者读得愉快），再发展到"三之"（知之，好之，乐之）目的论。这就是中国学派的文学翻译理论发展为"美化之艺术"（"三美"，"三化"，"三之"的艺术）的概况。

许渊冲

2011年10月

图书在版编目（CIP）数据

唐诗三百首: 汉英对照 / 许渊冲译. —2版. — 北京: 五洲传播出版社,
2018.8（2022.10重印）
（许译中国经典诗文集）
ISBN 978-7-5085-4027-6

Ⅰ.①唐… Ⅱ.①许… Ⅲ.①汉语－英语－对照读物
②唐诗－诗集 Ⅳ.①H319.4：I

中国版本图书馆CIP数据核字(2018)第198825号

唐诗三百首

译　　者：许渊冲
策划编辑：荆孝敏　郑　磊
责任编辑：王　峰
中文编辑：孟学文
英文编辑：杨贤茂　郁　辉
装帧设计：北京正视文化艺术有限责任公司
出版发行：五洲传播出版社
地　　址：北京市海淀区北三环中路31号生产力大楼B座6层
邮　　编：100088
电　　话：010-82005927，010-82007837
网　　址：http://www.cicc.org.cn　http://www.thatsbooks.com
印　　刷：北京市房山腾龙印刷厂
版　　次：2012年1月第1版　2022年10月第2版第8次印刷
开　　本：140mm×210mm　1/32
印　　张：11.75
字　　数：300千字
书　　号：ISBN 978-7-5085-4027-6
定　　价：98.00元